Generous Heart

A Daily Prayer Book

Donal Neary SJ

Messenger MJP Publications

Published by Messenger Publications, 2025

The right of Donal Neary SJ to be identified as the author of the Work has been asserted by him in accordance with the Copyright and Related Rights Act, 2000. All rights reserved. No part of this book may be reproduced or utilised in any form or by any means electronic or mechanical including photography, filming, recording, video recording, photocopying or by any information storage and retrieval system or shall not by way of trade or otherwise be lent, resold or otherwise circulated in any form of binding or cover other than that in which it is published without prior permission in writing from the publisher.

Scripture quotations are taken from the New Revised Standard Version Updated Edition. Copyright © 2021 National Council of Churches of Christ in the United States of America. Used by permission. All rights reserved worldwide.

'A word from the *Messenger*' taken from the *Sacred Heart Messenger*. To subscribe go to www.messenger.ie

ISBN 978-1-7881-2751-6

Designed by Brendan McCarthy
Typeset in Adobe Caslon Pro & Adobe Garamond Pro
Printed by Hussar Books

Messenger MJP Publications

Milltown Park,
Dublin, D06W9Y7
Ireland
www.messenger.ie

O Sacred Heart of Jesus,
I place all my trust in thee.

Table Of Contents

Introduction 07
How to use this book 09
A reflection on the generous heart of Jesus 11

1: In the morning 13
2: During the day 49
3: At night 91
4: The Examen 135

Notes from my prayer 138

Introduction

I got my start working on a school magazine. I have had an on-and-off-again relationship with publishing ever since. My first article for the *Messenger* was published in 1967. I wrote on St Paul. Quite a feat for an amateur writer in early Jesuit life! Since then I have published my own books and at one stage co-edited an inter-seminary magazine with the late Redemptorist Fr Raphael Gallagher. And of course, since 2014 I have been the editor of the *Sacred Heart Messenger*, one of Ireland's best-selling religious magazines.

I remember when the cover of the *Messenger* changed. For decades it had been the same image of the Sacred Heart every month. Then the decision was made to change to a different image of a religious nature each month, and then finally to a variety of images of all kinds. How we all agonised over the decision! We were warned there could be *severe repercussions* for the circulation of the magazine. Despite the changes, the familiar red of the magazine has remained. The severe repercussions never materialised.

In Ireland and abroad the *Messenger* is iconic. One reader told me that she kept the *Messenger* in the car for safe driving! The circulation of the magazine peaked at over 200,000 during the Second World War, or 'the Emergency' as it was called in Ireland. This was in part because the then editor had bought a great store of paper just before the outbreak of the war. The *Messenger* was one of the few periodicals that could continue despite the paper shortages. It has been in continuous circulation since 1888.

Over the years the articles became more varied in content. Frs Paul Leonard, Paddy Carberry, Brendan Murray and myself – all successors of the late long-time editor Fr Charles Scantlebury

– did our best to make it a magazine truly devoted to 'making known the love of God in the heart of Jesus' with articles relevant to the Church in the world.

This book, *Generous Heart*, collects more than a decade's worth of my reflections for the *Messenger*, very much rooted in the Ignatian spirituality of finding God in ordinary life. The Apostleship of Prayer, now the Pope's Worldwide Prayer Network, is close to my heart too, and the *Messenger* continues to bring the pope's monthly prayer intentions into the homes of thousands of readers. It's in small ways that faith grows! Daily prayer is part of that. I hope *Generous Heart* will bring something of this 'modern message in a much-loved tradition' into your heart.

The *Messenger* has been a constant in my Jesuit life, a constant I am very pleased with. It was also a constant in my family life as for many years my mother was a promoter. She was responsible for over a hundred subscribers!

While it is an interesting and enjoyable job, I am aware it could not be done without the devotion of promoters, priests and parish helpers and personnel, and the work of our staff, and of course the support of our 21,000+ subscribers. A survey has shown that every magazine sold has an average of 2.4 readers. So I am grateful to our roughly 50,000 yearly readers all over the world.

I pray, offering Mass twice a week, in gratitude for all who in these and other ways support the *Messenger*. I thank you all most sincerely. Long may we pray together and spread devotion to the love of God in the heart of Christ.

Donal Neary SJ
28/07/2025

How to use this book

This book is designed to help you with daily prayer. Maybe you pray each and every day. Maybe you struggle to find the time to pray. In his introduction to the Sacred Space *Prayerbook* for 2026, Brendan Comerford SJ writes,

> In a letter addressed to the Jesuit Antonio Brandão, 1 June 1551, Ignatius writes, 'The scholastics can exercise themselves in seeking the presence of God our Lord in all things – for example, in conversing with one another, in walking, looking, hearing, thinking and in every thing they do.'
> Look at the marvellous freedom Ignatius gives to Jesuit scholastics as regards the form of prayer they might use. Ignatius knows that he is writing to busy people. He knows that it's next to impossible for full-time students to engage in long meditations or contemplations. So, almost anything they do, think, desire or feel can potentially be a prayer acceptable to God! Even a chat you've had with someone can, on reflection, be a source of prayer.

The idea here is the same. At any moment throughout your day, you can take some time to pray, and ordinary things – conversations, feelings, small acts of kindness – can be occasions for that prayer. In *Generous Heart*, you'll find reflections inspired by my ten years as editor of the *Sacred Heart Messenger*, still Ireland's best-selling Catholic magazine. In the morning, during the day and at night, they encourage you to find God in your day-to-day life. In each reflection, 'something to pray and think about' will be highlighted. An inspiring word from the *Messenger* is also included, drawn from the many writers who have contributed to the magazine during my time as editor.

In the morning, select a morning prayer. After saying your morning prayer, select a morning reflection. After reading it, take some time to dwell on 'something to think and pray about this morning'. You can make notes on what has come up for you in prayer during the morning using the note section at the back of this book.

During the day, select a daytime prayer. Make some time during the day, at lunchtime for example, to say your prayer, then select a daytime reflection. After reading it, take some time to dwell on 'something to think and pray about today'. You can make notes on what has come up for you in prayer during the day using the note section at the back of this book.

At night, select a nighttime prayer. After saying your prayer, select a nighttime reflection. After reading it, take some time to dwell on 'something to think and pray about tonight'. You can make notes on what has come up for you at night using the note section at the back of this book.

At the end of each day, you can follow Ignatius of Loyola in praying the Examen. A brief guide to the Examen can be found at the back of this book.

A reflection on the generous heart of Jesus

'Sacred Heart o' Jesus, take away our hearts o' stone, and give us hearts o' flesh!' These words from Seán O'Casey's *Juno and the Paycock* are an indication of the place of the Sacred Heart devotion in Irish faith. A favourite short prayer goes 'Sacred Heart of Jesus, I place all my trust in thee.'

A fervent devotee used to say, 'You can't beat the Sacred Heart for a favour.' At a time when God was portrayed as a distant figure in the sky, the Sacred Heart devotion brought him right into the hearts and homes of us all. That devotion made God very ordinary in Jesus!

The heart of Jesus is a generous heart; it is for all of us and for creation. Some energy flows from our devotion to his heart. As Pope Francis puts it in his encyclical *Dilexit Nos*, 'Christ's love can give a heart to our world and revive love wherever we think that the ability to love has been definitively lost' (*DN*, 218).

The title of Carson McCullers's novel *The Heart Is a Lonely Hunter* comes from the idea of the heart always searching. Maybe it's a title we could identify with. We might even connect it with the Sacred Heart. We hunt and search for love within marriage, family and friendships. At times the search can be frustrating. It was frustrating for Jesus too. He looked over Jerusalem and wondered what more he could do to show love. It must have been lonely for him; he was so often misunderstood and rejected, and finally he was put to death.

Jesus is a 'hunter'. He hunts for us, finding us, feeding us, bringing us home. As he hunts for us, we hunt for him. Often we miss him, not realising that his love is very near to us in the people we meet, in our varied experiences and in the beauty of creation.

I hope that this book will help you both to seek and be found by Jesus in your daily prayer.

Something to think and pray about
The heart of Jesus is a generous heart.

A word from the *Messenger*
'Devotion to the Sacred Heart need not be an exercise in nostalgia. It still has the power to tap into that encounter with Jesus Christ, the merciful face of God, which is such good news for all humankind and for our planet. The blood and water that flowed from the pierced side of Jesus (Jn 19:34) continues to be the source of healing and fullness of life for our world.' – Gerry O'Hanlon SJ, 'The Sacred Heart Today', June 2023

1. In the morning

Morning Prayers

I rise up with God,
may he rise up with me.
May his arm be around me,
waking, working and sleeping.
May I bring God's love and grace
to all I meet this day and receive
that grace from them.
Amen.

With an open heart,
may I receive your joy, peace, energy and compassion.
With open hands,
may I receive your anointing,
to bring his Word and mercy to all I meet.
With an open mind,
may I receive the meaning of life,
which you offer today and always.
Amen.

1. In the morning

Father of Mercy,
you have brought me to the dawning of a new day.
I recognise your goodness to me.
Help me to walk with you in friendship,
working with you for the benefit of my brothers and sisters across the world.
Amen.

Heavenly Father,
I thank you for my life.
Life is not always easy and cheerful,
but with the help of the Holy Spirit that you sent,
it is full of meaning.
Help me to work well and to fulfil the tasks that are expected of me.
May I also bring joy to all that I do and fill others with that joy.
Amen.

1. In the morning

Father, here I am.
I know you are always with me.
I place my heart in the heart of your Son, Jesus,
who gives himself to us in the Eucharist each day.
May your Holy Spirit make me his friend and his apostle,
available for his mission of compassion.
I place in your hands my joys and hopes,
my works and sufferings,
everything I am and have.
Amen.

Lord God, receive me on this day
and hear my morning prayer.
Bless my parents, family, friends, teachers and all those who love
and care for me.
Bless me also and protect me from danger today.
Give me strength to be truthful, honest, kind and helpful
to others.
Amen.

1. In the morning

Dawn

~~~

Each year at dawn on the morning of 21 December, a group walks through Newgrange, the neolithic passage tomb in County Meath, and, weather permitting, is rewarded with the sight of the sun reaching right into the tomb.

Even on normal days, Newgrange is memorable. How much more so on the longest night of the year! Dating from about 3000 BC, older than the Pyramids of Giza, burials took place in the tomb, and it was designed in such a way for light to reach the centre of the tomb even today, after three millennia. It is a tribute to natural wonder; and at a deeper level, it is a sustained moment of faith in the divine, in mystery, in the creator God.

The tomb at Newgrange is as dark as many a person's life in illness, depression, poverty, as dark as the life of one who has lost meaning, loved ones, hope.

The Bible often mentions light: Isaiah says, 'The people who walked in darkness have seen a great light' (Ps 9:2). Jesus describes himself as 'the light of the world' (Jn 8:12). He is as essential to our life and world as the light is to each day.

The light that reaches into the tomb cannot be destroyed. It is always near, even when the clouds are at their thickest.

Many need the light of Christ. He depends on you to switch on his light for people near and dear to you and those far away.

The light will shine into the deepest part of the tomb in Newgrange; may the light of God shine where it is most needed today. 'In your light, we see light' (Ps 36).

1. In the morning

Something to think and pray about this morning
Jesus is as essential to my life as the light is to each day.

A word from the *Messenger*
'Our ancestors learned to use stone about 7,000 years ago. This is called the neolithic or New Stone Age (*lithos* = 'stone' in Greek). Newgrange dates from this period; later came the Pyramids. Having waited a long time, stone became the basis of civilisation. Think of the great cities that sprinkle the globe, the billions of homes made from stone, the vast interlacing of roads that enables travel and transport. Think also of your local street … We do well to grow silent before rocks, cliffs, pebbles, stones and concrete. Then chat them up by imagining their story. Every stone has a long history; every gravestone hints at the world beyond. For theologian Leonardo Boff, hills and mountains hint at God; they support, endure and welcome everything, and God behaves in the same way. Stones, like leaves, point quietly to their maker!' – Brian Grogan SJ, 'Finding God in a Stone', March 2023

1. In the morning

Looking Ahead

Some of the words of Jesus seem stark: not preferring mother and father to Jesus; about how in caring for others, you care for Jesus; how in your neglect of others, you neglect him. When God is central to your life, however, love can be found in the smallest acts of service, like offering a cup of water.

Jesus is not outside human relationships. His needs are found in the real needs of ordinary people. You give a cup of water to the person who needs it. The God in one person helps the God in another. This is the central point of faith.

You can help in simple ways. Pope Francis refers to this in his encouragement of simple love: 'It is like the warm supper we look forward to at night, the early lunch awaiting someone who gets up early to go to work. Homely gestures. Like a blessing before we go to bed, or a hug after we return from a hard day's work. Love is shown by little things, by attention to small daily signs which make us feel at home. Faith grows when it is lived and shaped by love' (Closing Mass for the Eighth World Meeting of Families, Philadelphia, September 2015).

In prayer, you might recall a time when someone helped you in a small or big way. You can recall and relive the experience and let your gratitude be part of your prayer.

You can in prayer offer yourself to do the same, as you look ahead to the coming day. You can imagine the people you may meet and pray for them, or situations you may face in which you will need God's help.

You can recall the words of the Lord: 'whatever you do for the least of these brothers or sisters of mine, you do for me' (Mt 25).

1. In the morning

Something to think and pray about this morning
I will give a cup of water to someone who needs it.

A word from the *Messenger*
'I came to know myself as I really am: human, limited, weak and dependent. Through that experience, I also came to know God. It changed my notion of prayer. Walking the Camino reminds me of how I truly am before God: not in control, naked, unadorned and in need of help. Only through being open and trusting, handing it over, am I free of fear and open to receive God's gifts.' – Brendan McManus SJ, 'Trust on the Journey', July 2024

1. In the morning

Mystery

A group of youngsters, we were waiting for the arrival of the bishop. As altar servers, we always loved to ask him if he could explain the Trinity. We didn't have any theological interest in the question. We just loved the way he said with reverence and mockery of us, 'It's a mystery.' When he went, one of us would inevitably say, 'We got him to say it again!'

No matter how you put it, the life of the Father, Son and Holy Spirit together is a mystery: a truth to be meditated on and enjoyed but never understood.

Much of the best of life is shrouded in mystery: the gasp of joy and wonder at the birth of a child, the pondering of what we cannot grasp, the love that starts and grows, and the mystery of marriage and family. We end our lives with the greatest mystery of all, death, and then the mystery of eternal life. Mystery is not a problem to be solved but a question to pour over.

Some mysteries can overwhelm us, like the death of loved ones, illnesses and broken relationships. They are mysteries that we bring to our God, who is Mystery in love, forgiveness and three Persons.

As you look forward to the day, maybe you are anxious about the challenges ahead. Can you accept that some of the best of life is mysterious, beyond your control? Maybe you can be glad of the mystery and how there is always something more in life.

The bishop let us know that what we liked to hear him say was worth the saying.

If you can say it, you can live it!

Something to think and pray about this morning
There is always something more in life.

A word from the *Messenger*
'Praying is one of the most typical human activities that exists. Those who pray desire to open themselves to the mystery of God's presence. The praying person desires to be receptive to the love that God is and that he wants to share with people on an ongoing basis. Prayer is eminently relational.' – Nikolaas Sintobin SJ, 'What Is Praying?', February 2025

1. In the morning

Vocation

At eighty-seven years of age, Fr Matt has been a diocesan priest for over sixty-three years. He has been living in a large, sprawling urban parish for twenty-one years, where he retired at seventy-five, and he loves it. Recently, I asked him what he was doing now. Though he is in excellent health, I would have expected him to be mostly retired, enjoying his hobbies and his memories, and maybe doing some light pastoral work in the parish. His answer still amazes me! Apart from writing a new book, his third in a few years, he says a daily Mass in the parish, at least two at the weekend and every third Sunday he preaches at five Masses and visits the sick and housebound in his area with a 'younger assistant' of over seventy!

As Matt says, 'We promised to give our all!' Indeed he does! That's something about vocation. It's more than a job for him and always has been. In a life where he enjoyed travel, reading, friendship and conversation, he has not lost sight of the core of his life and being. Many are like him, not only priests. To enjoy the core of your life's calling is a huge consolation, as St Ignatius would call it. It's what gives meaning and joy to so many husbands and wives, to life-long partners, to family carers and to grandparents. It is the difference between vocation and a job.

The commitment of healthcare workers, teachers, school- and health-chaplains, service providers of all sorts comes from a core commitment to the common good and to love and service. Fr Matt highlights something of the meaning of priesthood and its call of service and love, of joy and commitment. Like all who live like that, he has a sense of humour, one of Pope Francis's conditions for holiness. While I hope that many will follow him as priests, I take the example of his life as being wider than any one way of following a core calling. It is a spur and encouragement to everyone to live out their vocation.

Whether you are a teenager or a young eighty-something or somewhere in between, ask yourself this morning what God is calling you to do today.

Something to think and pray about this morning
God encourages me to live out my vocation.

A word from the *Messenger*
'Our youth have come of age during a time of major technological change. They have grown up with the internet and all the social media platforms and outlets that have evolved. They seem to live much of their life "online". In the midst of this chaotic world, how many of them really get an opportunity to reflect on the key vocational questions? How can they be expected to reflect on their relationship with God when some of them are unsure who God is?' – Gerard Gallagher, 'Youth Synod', May 2018

1. In the morning

Family of Listeners

There was a time when you 'got Mass' (that is, fulfilled your obligation) if you got in by the Offertory! The first part – the liturgy of the Word, in Latin of course – was then considered of little relevance in the Roman Catholic tradition. Today the presence of God is highlighted both in the Eucharist and in the Word. The Word of God prepares you to receive the bread of life. This recalls one of the principal statements of the Second Vatican Council: 'The proclamation of God's Word at the celebration entails an acknowledgement that Christ himself is present, that he speaks to us, and that he wishes to be heard' (*Verbum Domini*, 56).

In the reading of the Word, Christ himself is the speaker! Many Mass-goers and even a few priests will be glad that Pope Francis warns against improvising or giving 'long, pedantic homilies or wandering off into unrelated topics'. In other words, don't bore the congregation, rouse them to enthusiasm about their faith!

The Word of God can be a daily practice. Some read the gospel for each day, using, for example, the Sacred Space *Prayerbook*. The reading of the day's gospel doesn't end with reading. For Pope Francis 'the great challenge before us in life [is] to listen to Sacred Scripture and then practise mercy'.

Prayerfully reading the message and life of Jesus in the Gospels encourages you and challenges you to follow the Word. Jesus said, 'My mother and my brothers are those who hear the Word of God and do it' (Lk 8:21). That's you and me, the family of listeners.

As you get ready this morning, make a commitment to read today's gospel, listen to the Word and then get out and practise mercy.

Something to think and pray about this morning
The Word of God is a daily practice.

A word from the *Messenger*
'There is a biblical belief in divine grace, divine compassion. There is no belief in abiding and consuming divine anger. What is often proclaimed of love, famously in the refrain of Psalm 136 – "for his steadfast love endures forever" – is never said about anger. The normal and original attitude of God is love and mercy.' – Wilfrid Harrington OP, 'The Mystery of God', May 2019

1. In the morning

Baptism

I attended a Mass at Dublin church for all those who had been baptised there over the years. I had been baptised there seventy-four years ago!

During the Mass, I thought of my parents and godparents – my godmother always remembered the big occasions of my youth, but my godfather conveniently forgot birthdays! Baptism brought me into a new bond with my first family. It also introduced me to the community of the Church where I have found guidance, support in prayer, a space of hope and refreshment and of forgiveness. In this community, I have made many friends, as a teenager and as an adult, that have lasted over the years. Baptism has given me a link of hope with those gone before me. I am thankful for it.

A homily during that Mass gave me a good image of the lasting grace of baptism. I pictured myself as a five-day-old baby wrapped in the shawl of God's love and protection, and realised that that protection has been with me all my life. In baptism, God promises his love and protection for always. The ceremony may be for the day, but the sacrament is for always.

This morning, can you recall your baptism and give joyful thanks for it? Perhaps you too could pay a visit to the church where you were baptised and visualise the ceremony and remember the people who welcomed you into the Church.

For all the difficulties in church life, I am glad to be part of it. As is said at the ceremony, 'This is our faith, and we are proud to profess it in Christ Jesus our Lord.'

Something to think and pray about this morning
In baptism, God promises his love and protection to me for always.

A word from the *Messenger*
'In baptism we partake in the wonders of the life of faith. As we grow and mature, we make our own the gift of faith that we have received, as we witness to the love and hope that only Christ can offer.' – Fr Albert McDonnell, 'The Gift of Baptism', August 2023

1. In the morning

Patience

～✤～

I was passing through a shopping centre in Dublin in October, and I thought to myself is it Halloween already? Children around me were already in their costumes, even though the holiday itself was days away! I was treated to the strange, modern sight of children in Halloween costumes wandering past shelves full of Christmas merchandise. It was then I knew I lived in a culture that found it hard to wait, that needed immediate gratification.

I remember a time when turkey was just for Christmas, and hot cross buns just for Good Friday. Carols were kept for Christmas Masses, and the Alleluia chorus for Easter.

I think people have lost the experience of anticipation, and find waiting makes them uneasy. Yet much of the best of life is about waiting! There is joy in anticipating the family coming home for Christmas or St Patrick's Day. And then there is the waiting that you don't have control over: the birth of a child or the death of a loved one.

You can learn a lot in patient waiting. Consolation comes and goes in God's own time. But faith waits. Love can be a waiting game too, as you allow loved ones to grow up, mourn or open up to trust.

As you look to the day ahead, can you try and be more patient in life? After all if you are not accustomed to waiting for the ordinary things of life, how will you be able to wait in patience for the best? The seed will grow, and the resurrection will come. Is it worth the wait? I think so.

1. In the morning

Something to think and pray about this morning
If I am not accustomed to waiting for the ordinary things, how will I wait in patience for the best?

A word from the *Messenger*
'Patience allows us to accept without anxiety or resentment the truth that life will not necessarily unfold according to our plan or within our timescale. From the perspective of faith, patience includes trusting that God is ultimately in control and his purposes for creation will be accomplished. The challenge for everyone is: do I really believe this?' – Shane Daly SJ, 'Patience and the Spiritual Life', January 2019

1. In the morning

Always Open

You can put it like this. Jesus left the tomb and was clothed in his risen body. You and I and the Church are Jesus' new risen body. And he likes all the different parts of his new body: people of all different colours and ages, people of sin and sanctity. The focus is not on the tomb, because it is empty! Jesus has moved on, and his focus is elsewhere.

Someone said to me in my parish, 'I love passing your church. The door is always open.' At the end of Mass, the door is always open to let people out to spread the message of the risen Lord. Among the most important words of the Mass are 'Go now and serve the Lord with your lives.' A church community with an eye only on heaven lives only half the truth. The Church is called to go out to the edge, to the outsider, the sinner, those nobody wants.

The clothing of Christ's followers is well described by St Paul: 'Clothe yourselves with compassion, kindness, humility, meekness and patience. Bear with one another and, if anyone has a complaint against another, forgive each other; just as the Lord has forgiven you, so you also must forgive. Above all, clothe yourselves with love. And be thankful' (Col 3:12–15).

St Ignatius is said to have asked each morning 'Who can I help today?' This morning, say to yourself, 'If I can help somebody along the way, then my life will not be in vain.' Jesus might say that if you can help someone today, then his rising has not been in vain. The Resurrection is about how you live in this life. It is the mystery of the new life of Jesus that sends you out into the world.

Christians are a grateful people, clothed in Christ as in the baptismal robe. This gratitude gives you the warmth and security you need to be the Body of Christ today.

1. In the morning

Something to pray and think about this morning
Who can I help today?

A word from the *Messenger*
'The best way of responding to forgiveness is by extending forgiveness to others. In Matthew's parable of the unmerciful servant (Mt 18:13–35), we meet again the sinner and his God. An impossible debt is casually written off in response to the sinner's plea, but when the recipient of such forgiveness cannot find it in his heart to be merciful, the master is "angry". Response to God's gracious forgiveness cannot be payment of a debt that is already fully remitted. It is, instead, warm thanks given for the blessing of such forgiving love and readiness to be forgiving in our turn.' – Wilfrid Harrington OP, 'Forgiveness', June 2019

1. In the morning

Walking Together

On meeting a colleague recently, what I hoped would be a friendly conversation turned out to be a lecture! Maybe you have had a similar experience: you tentatively made an observation on some issue and were treated to a lecture from on high! Little conversation, little listening.

In a call to Jesuits in Lithuania, Pope Francis asked them to help him build a new Church. The characteristics of this new Church would be dialogue, listening, nearness and journey. We converse, giving each other time. We listen as best we can. In this sort of conversation, we are near to each other and to the Spirit of God. He reminds us that 'unless we listen, all our words will be nothing but useless chatter' (*Gaudete et Exsultate*, 150). The pope highlights that we are on a journey together, none of us having it all together and adds that 'when someone has an answer for everything, it is a sign they are not on the right road' (*Gaudete et Exsultate*, 41). This is the deep spiritual renewal he hopes for in the Church, which is to be centred only on Jesus Christ. He said to the group of forty-one Jesuits, some of whom had been imprisoned during the communist regime, 'I don't know what to ask from you specifically. But what needs to be done today is to accompany the Church in a deep spiritual renewal. I believe the Lord wants a change in the Church. I have said many times that a perversion of the Church today is clericalism. But fifty years ago the Second Vatican Council said this clearly: the Church is the People of God.'

This morning take some time to appreciate the challenge of walking together as one body in the Church, truly listening to one another. Ask yourself if the people in your church community are being heard and if you are journeying with them. Remember, you are a part of the People of God, and you are needed if the Church is to discern what God wants of the Church today.

Something to think and pray about this morning
If I have an answer for everything, it is a sign I am on the wrong road.

A word from the *Messenger*
'*Conversing*: etymologically, *con-* means "meeting", "aggregation" or "corporation", while the Latin *versare* means "to go around". What these approximations make clear is that the purpose of conversation is *cooperative*: that is, all who engage in it are able to win; and all share a world, collaborate or join together in exploring a theme. Using another image, we can say that *conversing* is like a pouring together into a common stream or watercourse, transforming individuals into community. As the *Final Document* puts it, "conversion is at play in conversation".'
– Juan A. Guerrero Alves SJ & Óscar Martín López SJ, *Conversation in the Spirit* (2025)

1. In the morning

Breakfast

You can sometimes try too hard. The impact of Jesus, risen from the dead, was felt in small ways. He listened to two people on the road and broke bread with them, and so they believed. He called someone by her name, and she believed. He shared fish with his disciples on the shores of the Sea of Galilee, and they believed. No big lectures, no astounding apparitions. Resurrection happened in a garden they all knew, in the houses they lived in, at the lake side where they grew up.

Jesus' last meal with the disciples was breakfast at dawn (Jn 21:1–14). So ordinary! The bread of the earth becomes the bread of heaven. It is a meal shared as food for the journey of spreading the kingdom of God.

Faith grows in small ways mostly. You take a few minutes every day at some fixed time to pray and be with God. You decide to be kinder to others, to thank God for someone when you feel unkind towards them. You find the great in the small. You find the risen Lord in the ordinary and in others.

This morning over breakfast take a moment to be thankful for the meal, the morning and the day ahead.

Something to think and pray about this morning
Faith grows in small ways.

A word from the *Messenger*
'The kingdom of God is a seed that falls on various kinds of terrain, some fruitful and others not. It's wheat among weeds. It's like a mustard seed or leaven hidden in dough. The kingdom is small and often undiscernible in its early stages but over time will grow to full fruition.' – David Breen, 'A Treasure and a Pearl', April 2025

1. In the morning

Mrs Hope

Growing up, Mrs Hope was my next-door neighbour. Each New Year's Eve at twelve, she would carry a lump of burning coal into her house and roar out 'Happy New Year, Wilfrid Road.' She was always a jolly person. Her New Year's Eve greeting fitted her name; there was something of friendliness and good wishes and New Year's hope about her.

A new beginning gives you a lift, bringing with it a sense of expectation. It reminds you that life moves on. What is good may get better, and tough times may pass. Hope is a gift of God, which you can call into each new day. Maybe you can make a wish as you read this that everyone you meet today – good friends, family members, even those who cause you difficulty – will find prosperity, peace and happiness.

The Church calls for renewal. The Church wants to renew its commitment to those on the margins of society, to care for those without homes, without decent medical care, for refugees and asylum seekers and for the elderly and unborn. Pray this morning that the life and enthusiasm in the Church of different parish groups will increase, creating communities both of hope and of compassionate care.

You need the companionship and love of family, friends and faith. You need to carry the hope of new beginnings and of renewal through the whole year. I like that my neighbour's name was Mrs Hope. She shared her hope through the whole year with everyone on the road. She was full of good humour, help in the small things of family life and love of the children of Wilfrid Road. A lady of hope indeed!

1. In the morning

Something to think and pray about this morning
I bring God's gift of hope into my day.

A word from the *Messenger*
'The Christian community is to be the living witness everywhere of God's everlasting love and of hope for our eternal future. The Church is *the* pilgrim of hope, on its way but not yet arrived. And despite all our shortcomings, we are the divine workforce. The Church can come across as weak and fragmented, but when people cry "God, where are you?", we can point to its vast service of the world in its closeness to the needy, its defence of the dignity of all, its intercessory prayer and worship, its missionary effort to be the Good News for everyone. We are the divine plan on legs.' – Brian Grogan SJ, 'Beacon of Hope', March 2025

1. In the morning

First Easter Morning

—⊷✦⊶—

I sometimes wonder what the first Easter morning was like to experience. It seemed a quiet time, and the Gospels present a lot of doubt regarding it: no Alleluias were sung, no Easter cake was eaten, no Easter garden blessing! There was, however, a lot of sadness as the women wandered to the tomb to anoint Jesus' body. Then, later in the morning, the story of the two disciples on the Emmaus journey played out. Easter is a journey, not a one-day event. The faith of the followers developed gradually over time. In Jesus, who listened keenly to all those who shared their story with him, they found faith.

Much deepening of faith comes from the experience of others, as was the case with Thomas finding faith and the Emmaus disciples. It is a journey of discovery from sadness to joy, from doubt to faith, from disillusionment to confidence. And it is a long one made among peers. It brings challenges akin to those of Thomas: you wander away from the community and then return, all leading ultimately to your own personal confession of faith.

Various occasions in life serve to deepen faith. Maybe a child's First Communion or a grandchild's baptism can call you further into faith. Perhaps a bereavement could lead to the discovery of a 'dark love of faith', resulting in some comfort. Illness and death can spur faith too; in fear, some sense the outstretched, wounded hand of the risen Lord! Maybe you have been badly hurt in life, and somehow you find the strength to pray for the person who harmed you, in turn allowing you to find some freedom to heal. Of course, you may fall in love, make a long-term commitment and find faith through a beautiful new relationship.

This morning, as on that first Easter morning, the door to faith is wide open. The Lord knocks on your door and asks to come

1. In the morning

into your life to love you just as you are. Just think, where and in whom will you meet Jesus today?

Something to think and pray about this morning
My faith is a long journey of discovery.

A word from the *Messenger*
'Using our gifts to help others can give us a deep sense of purpose and self-worth. Choosing achievable goals and engaging in activities that connect us to a sense of purpose can assist us to move forward in life with belief in a positive future. Connecting to others as well as participating in faith-based communities may introduce us to people who share our values and understand and empathise with us. This can deepen our meaningful relationships and bring us important validation that can greatly enrich our lives.' – Tina McGrath, 'Mental Health and Faith', December 2020

1. In the morning

The Rising Sun

The Easter mystery continues every day in the Church. In the eucharistic prayer at each Mass, we commemorate the death and resurrection of the Lord. It can be good to look at the events of Easter all through the year, like the situation of the women who came to the tomb.

They were confused as they came there laden with the ointments: How would they get to the body of Jesus to show him this respect? Who would roll away the stone?

In the rising sun, it dawned on them that something very strange and unusual had happened. The stone was rolled away.

Soon they would see him. They would go ahead into Galilee. They would be the first proclaimers of the Resurrection. But did they often remember their journey to the tomb?

The event reached into their ordinary lives. They probably realised that many stones in their lives had been rolled away.

The same is true for you. Think of the burdens you carry in your life: the memories that stir pain, the grief that lasts, ill health, worries about family, bereavement and many others. In the loving power of God, in sharing faith and difficulties with others, in the real hope that God is always near, your stones are rolled away.

In love Jesus rolls away your stones.

A stone often has a crack, and a little flower can grow through it. Through cracks in the stones of your life, light and healing breaks through. The women at the tomb realised that morning that love was around them. It just took awhile to believe. It can be the same for you.

1. In the morning

Something to think and pray about this morning
Jesus rolls away my stone.

A word from the *Messenger*
'In Matthew's Gospel, Mary Magdalene and the other Mary are the central witnesses in the passion and resurrection narratives. They had seen Jesus die and watched him being buried (27:57, 61). Now they are the first witnesses to Jesus' resurrection. Together they meet the Jewish requirement that everything had to be established by two or three witnesses. The unexpected detail is that in choosing the first witnesses to Jesus' resurrection, God chose women, subverting the cultural belief that the testimony of women was unreliable. It also argues for the historical truth of the Resurrection, because if it were a later creation of the Church, as some assert, the primary witnesses would have been male.' – David Breen, 'Easter in Matthew', April 2023

1. In the morning

Christian Vocation

If you take a good look at the life of Jesus, you will notice him as a man of presence, prayer, teaching and of care for the poor. You see that in how often the Gospels present him as being with people, a man among men and women, attractive and selfless. His presence was often a teaching presence, as he taught people about God the Father and how to live. He was a man of prayer, both personal, as he spent hours in prayer alone, and communal, as he worshipped in the synagogue. His eye always went for the poor, and his heart went out to help them; he was concerned for them and encouraged his followers to be on the side of those who were poor, neglected and sinful.

Jesus in his way of life gives a clue as to what the Church and parish might be in the future.

The parish is a people of prayer and liturgy, who study and learn about faith, who look out for each other in the ordinary cares and difficulties of life, and who care for and help the poor in the locality and the poor of the wider world.

I've often heard parishioners talk in this way about their parish priests: 'He always had a kind word when we met him on the street.' 'We met him often around the parish, maybe walking the dog; he was there for us at bad times like illnesses and funerals.' They also often ask a priest something like 'I don't go to the church much, but would you pray for my aunt who is very ill?' A priest and parish do their best to create and celebrate liturgy – Mass, funerals, weddings and other occasions – in a way that links into the lives of the people and enlivens their faith.

As you plan for the day ahead, think about these three calls: to be present for one another; to pray and learn; to care for the poor. Can you live these out today, as Jesus did, and make them your Christian vocation?

1. In the morning

Something to think and pray about this morning
I take a good look at the life of Jesus. What do I notice?

A word from the *Messenger*
'It takes time to discover who we are and who we need to be. It also takes time to figure out what we can do in life to express, sustain and flourish as the person we truly are and need to be. Who we truly are, is the person God calls us to be. This is the deepest sense of vocation: God calls us to become ourselves, "to have life, and have it to the full" (Jn 10:10). To lose sight of this is to lose sight of the living God who calls us into life and sustains us day in and day out.' – Archbishop Dermot Farrell, 'Hearing Our Call', April 2024

1. In the morning

Salvation for All

The saving love of Jesus on the cross continues through all time. You may wonder this morning what you need to be saved from today. Does knowing that Jesus is with you today help save you from fear and anxiety? He will walk with you today, bringing his saving love with him.

Jesus' salvation is for everyone. The world needs it just as much as you do. There is poverty, homelessness and violence, families living in hotels and the hardship of direct provision for many asylum seekers. These are tough times for young people who need confidence in their future.

Shepherds were the poorest and were Jesus' first visitors. The Gospel of Jesus saves the poor, and you save them with him.

Today can you look out for the people in your life? Can you look out for young people, who are so at risk of addiction and self-harm? Can you look out for the people on the streets who are in need? Can you help the prisoner, the migrant, the victim?

The saving work Jesus began with two ordinary people who had extraordinary love and faith: Mary and Joseph. The risen Lord invites you to be a partner in care. With you Jesus still saves the world.

1. In the morning

Something to think and pray about this morning
Jesus walks with me today.

A word from the *Messenger*
'Anxieties and fears can dominate us to such an extent that we are afraid to take a risk. There is a rule of thumb when thinking about abandoning the Camino: to get out the door the next day and walk a few kilometres at least. This often helps overcome negative thinking and empowers us to realise how much we can do. 'Always go', or at least 'try it and see', can be a helpful approach to living a more fulfilling pilgrim life in line with our deeper desires and hopefully with what God wants of us.' – Brendan McManus SJ, 'Always Go', December 2024

1. In the morning

Waking Up

Jesus was raised from the dead by the love and power of his father. He didn't just rise himself! He didn't say, 'Gosh that was a good sleep' and then get up! His resurrection was a totally new way of life.

This new life is symbolised by Jesus leaving his clothes behind. Peter, who did not believe Mary Magdalene, Joanna and the other women, saw the linen clothes and realised the truth (Lk 1:24–25). The promise Jesus made to rise from the dead had been fulfilled.

It's also interesting that when the Apostles met Jesus, after the Resurrection, they met him in the ordinary. They met him in a garden, as Mary Magdalene was maybe tidying and watering the flowers. They met him on a journey, a long walk of seven miles to Emmaus, two very disgruntled disciples. They went fishing, and they met him on the shore. He didn't give them a homily then. He just made them breakfast. The written life of Jesus is in the ordinary for him and for us.

You will find the Resurrection anytime you are uplifted in prayer and in love. When you work for the poor, for justice in the world, for peace, that is the risen love of the Lord. And the big gift of the risen Lord is peace. He so often said, 'Peace I leave with you' (Jn 14:27). The other big gift was his forgiveness.

This morning, as you wake up, open yourself to the life and the breath and the peace of the risen Lord.

1. In the morning

Something to think and pray about this morning
The Resurrection is a totally new way of life.

A word from the *Messenger*
'The two disciples [on the road to Emmaus] had a new spring in their step. They ignored the gathering dusk and ran back to Jerusalem to share the good news with their frightened companions. Jesus, who had disappeared before the meal was over, also went with them, unseen of course! He journeys with us and is often unrecognised as we walk our own Easter roads.' – Fr John Cullen, 'Word and Bread', March 2025

2: During the day

Daytime Prayers

God, our Father, I offer you my day.
I offer you my prayers, thoughts, words, actions, joys and sufferings
in union with your Son Jesus' heart,
for the salvation of the world. May the Holy Spirit,
who guided Jesus,
be my guide and my strength today,
so that I may witness to your love.
Amen.

Gracious God, thank you for the gift of today.
Refresh me.
Invite me to discover your presence in each person I meet
and every event that I encounter.
Teach me when to speak and when to listen.
When my day goes well, may I rejoice.
When it grows difficult, surprise me with new possibilities.
When life is overwhelming,
restore me to your peace and harmony.
May my living today reveal your goodness.
Amen.

2. During the day

You have made this day, O Lord.
May I spend it well in your service:
praying at all times,
serving your people,
who I meet this day with love and care.
Amen.

May I spend this day in faith
that you are with me in joy and sorrow,
love and friendship,
prayer and good works.
Lead me in the path of your love and your truth this day.
Amen.

Be with me Lord this day.
You are the light of the world to guide my decisions.
You are the Way, the Truth and the Life,
with me in all I do.
You are the Resurrection and Life, giving hope always.
Give joy and peace to all I meet this day.
Amen.

2. During the day

For what I have, I give thanks.
For what I need, I place myself into your hands, Lord.
Help me to see your face in all those I meet today
and to show them the same love that you have for me.
For all my faults and failings,
I am truly sorry,
and I commit to walking closer to the path you set out for me.
I unite myself with all those who are poor, ill or who are suffering this day.
May I experience the relief and healing I need
and be given a chance today to alleviate someone's else's pain in some small way.
Amen.

2. During the day

Everyday Kindness

There's something about kindness that spreads. Recently I thought my car had been stolen. I reported it to staff and to the gardaí. The next day I found it in the car park basement! I was humiliated. In those few hours I had great kindness from the car park attendants, who walked me through eight storeys of two car parks, and from the gardaí. There was no admonishment of my stupidity in not knowing where I had parked!

Often the same happens in small ways. You watch kindness or experience it: an elderly lady getting patient care from a bank official; the bus driver who stopped as I came to the bus after he started off; the teacher in school who never ridiculed any student, like myself, who stammered.

Kindness begets kindness. Kindness experienced leads to kindness spread. The kindness many experienced during Covid-19 spread from one to another as people collected groceries, rang each other up or kept in touch by email and Facebook and other sites. We visited when we could, and we prayed for each other.

Kindness is in the heart of God. There is the kindness of the Father in keeping us alive, and the kindness of the Son who walks with us every step of life's journey. The Spirit of kindness lives within each of us. The gate of heaven might have a poster: 'All who were kind in life, please enter here.'

It is not always easy. As Pope Francis remarked, 'Kindness is firm and persevering intention to always will the good of others, even the unfriendly.' We can add 'always want the best for others'. He also tweeted, 'Let us learn to live with kindness, to love everyone, even when they do not love us.' Kindness is in Paul's hymn to love: 'love is patient and kind' (1 Cor 13:4–8).

2. During the day

The poet Wordsworth wrote, 'The best portion of a good man's life is his little, nameless, unremembered acts of kindness and of love.' Little and nameless maybe, but I wonder is any kindness unremembered, even in the unconscious?

Whoever you are – car park attendant, garda, bus driver who waits when they needn't have and many more – thank you!

Something to think and pray about today
Kindness is in the heart of God.

A word from the *Messenger*
'Recently I have become very much aware of what I have tended to think of as the "small" blessings in my life. This, I think, I have done without adverting very much to their source. More recently, I have come to realise that these many gifts that I receive on a daily basis are what Dom Christopher Dillon, a monk of Glenstal Abbey, once described, when he wrote of "happy coincidences", as "God acting anonymously in the world." What a beautiful, true, inspiring and uplifting thought! The "small" blessings we receive on a daily basis have their source in a loving God who acts anonymously and with gentle and generous kindness in our world. His blessings to us are like prompts to remind us of his eternal and everlasting love for us.' – Aideen Madden, 'Small Blessings', September 2023

Listen

I can put my foot in it, as they say. After Mass in a hospital, a lady came up to me in a smart dressing gown and looking very well. Wanting to compliment her on how well she looked and her good health, I said, 'You're looking very well. You must be on the way out!' In a hospital setting, my compliment had a very different meaning than I intended!

Thankfully she had the good sense to laugh and ask, 'What do you mean?' I explained that I meant she would soon be going home. She, her son and I had a good laugh about it. It's just as well she asked me! I think her simple question 'What do you mean?' is actually a profound one.

How often do you presume you know what another person means? In dialogue over issues big and small, could you ask that question more often? What does the person with the opposite view to mine on politics, the Church, morality and other issues really mean? St Ignatius reminds his retreatants to 'put a good interpretation on what another says rather than the opposite'.

In debates with Lutherans during the Reformation, Ignatius recommended that the Jesuits look for what united rather than what divided. In a sincere search for truth, people listen to one another, debate, discern different opinions and then come to a decision.

The disciple of Jesus is a listener. Jesus meant for you to listen not only to his Word but to one another: 'Whoever is not against us is for us' (Mk 9:40). Listening is the key to peace among people. Listening is also the work of justice. Today can you look to the Gospel's most attentive listener, Mary, and try and listen as best you can to discover what people really mean?

Something to think and pray about today
I can't presume to know what others mean without first listening to them.

A word from the *Messenger*
'We can listen: listen to each other's concerns, listen in order to learn. This might mean taking a step back from our own agendas to go through the pain of really hearing where people are at in their own lives, staying with them and helping them feel that the Church cares about their joys, sorrows, fears and challenges.' – Patricia Carroll, 'Church of the Future', March 2019

2. During the day

Good Stories

The *Messenger* has been around for a while. There's a story that during the Second World War, when makeup was scarce, Irish women would rub the bright red cover of the *Messenger* on their faces to use as blush before a dance!

I must have heard that story a hundred times, but I always get a laugh from it. It's like a beloved family story. 'Ah go on Granny, tell us again the story of the night you thought lightning blew the roof off the house, and then it turned out to be your brother coming home late at night, making a racket!'

A good story is more than words. It's a memory of times gone by, of friends long since passed, and it has a personal meaning beyond the facts of its telling. Some people can make the greatest story boring, and others the most boring story interesting! The Gospels are full of stories. I can imagine someone saying to Peter, 'Tell us about the time you walked on water!' or to Mary, 'Tell us the one about when you went to the tomb.' The story comes to life because it is told from a place of faith and from an experience of the heart.

Each gospel story keeps alive the mystery and the meaning of an event in our salvation. The Gospel is the history of the past and the mystery of the present. The Word of Jesus is spoken for today. Ask yourself how the Gospel throws light on your life now and what it tells you about Jesus. Then the story will never be boring. It will leave more than a red mark on your cheek, but an imprint of love on your soul.

Something to think and pray about today
The Word of Jesus is spoken for today.

A word from the *Messenger*
'The entire Bible is a story of people in search of a home: Adam and Eve leave the garden; Noah and his family sail away from destruction; Abraham and Sarah follow God's call; Joseph and his band of brothers head to Egypt; Moses wanders through desert; Judah is exiled in Babylon. None of these people were going on a packaged holiday! Being displaced in exile and in the wilderness is part of the story of the Bible. It is an inherent part of belonging to God's people. For us, to be a Christian is to be en route, on the way, on a pilgrimage to a citizenship that is not situated right here.' – John Scally, 'His Own People Did Not Accept Him', February 2024

2. During the day

Lessons

I remember Agatha well, though I only met her on her deathbed. She was a patient in the Jesu Ashram hospital for the poor and destitute in Matigara, north-east India. The Jesu Ashram hospital was run by Jesuit brother Bob Mittelholz from Canada, who had joined the Jesuits after a successful business career. Agatha, from one of the poorest outlying villages, had been ill for some time and now asked for baptism. Hers was the Hindu faith, and for some reason she wished to join the faith of those who cared for her, mainly young nurses and doctors at the hospital.

On the night of the feast of St Agatha, we baptised her and named her after the saint. On her pillow we placed her baptismal candle and beside it the fruit she would bring to the gods, some apples and a banana. Years earlier that would have been seen as a pagan custom and been forbidden. Agatha went to God on 5 February 1982.

That evening has always remained with me. There is an afterglow of joy and insight in the experience. It was an unexpected and unusual experience for me, and in discernment I wondered what God was saying to me through it.

My faith was widened that night. Differences of religion seemed of little importance. At a time of death, I was open to joining the new faith of Agatha with the customs of her lifelong Hindu faith. The Spirit was working that night, and opened me up to an appreciation of God in many guises and rituals.

St Ignatius says that God teaches us 'as a schoolmaster teaches a pupil all our lives'. God is speaking to you through your experiences in life. Sometimes you miss the message, but other times you don't, and it makes a difference. Saints and holy people of all faiths can teach you about God.

Asking yourself what God has taught you today is a way of being surprised by God. So, what has God taught you today?

Something to think and pray about today
God teaches me as a pupil all my life.

A word from the *Messenger*
'Recently I perused Caravaggio's painting of the call of St Matthew. The painter has placed himself as Matthew the tax collector in the centre of the picture, a handsome, richly-robed man sitting with friends at his money table with a young boy leaning against his shoulder. Over in the shadows is the silhouette of Jesus. Matthew looks up, startled and incredulous, as he notices the beckoning finger of Jesus: "Who? Me? There must be some mistake!" St Peter protests with upraised hands against Jesus' action: "You cannot mean that man, Lord!" Jesus shocks and destabilises everyone in the picture: Matthew, his friends, young and old, and Peter. These moments when we are knocked off our balance, out of our routine and comfort zone, can be entry points for grace.' – Paul Andrews SJ, 'God of Surprises', May 2017

2. During the day

Gone Fishing

———✧———

Everything in life has something to teach us. In everything we can learn. There is formal learning, and there is learning about life in our hobbies and pastimes.

As a boy, I spent a lot of time fishing with a neighbour on the Liffey. We seldom caught much, a few perch and once a big pike. Most of us who fish know that reality.

Fishing can teach much. One lesson I got was patience. I kept throwing in the line and waited for a long time to maybe catch a fish. If I am a patient person, fishing taught me that. It taught me to wait for prayers to be answered and for good food to be cooked. The fish, once caught and brought home, needed time to cook, even at ten at night! Everything has its lesson.

Fishing brings us close to the divine. At a river for a long time, in a quiet place, we can find a space for God. Jesus knew when he called fishermen that he was calling people of reflection, patience, able to put up with disappointment when they caught no fish and generous in sharing the fish they brought home with their neighbours.

He knew also to link fishing with evangelisation – from now on, he said, it is people you will be catching (Lk 5:10).

Photography was also a favourite hobby of mine. If we go out to take photos, we notice much – it is called 'writing with light' – and so we become aware of the interplay of light and darkness in what we photograph.

The 'hobby' of sport is one of our greatest teachers – about teamwork, the joy of winning and the disappointment of losing, of being selected or dropped for the good of the team and much more. Everything in life is our teacher.

What we feel, hope for, let go of is part of discernment, of becoming clued in to what life teaches us. Much of it leads to gratitude, of how we are graced by God in both the joy and the sorrow of life.

We hope for what we do not see, and we wait for it with patience.

Something to think and pray about today
Everything has its lesson.

A word from the *Messenger*
'The word Jesus used in Luke 5:10 means to catch alive. It is used in the Septuagint for saving the lives of persons from danger (Num 31:15, 18; Deut 20:16). Those caught by the Lord and his disciples are caught for eternal life, unlike the fish, which are caught to be eaten.' – David Breen, 'The Call to Discipleship', February 2022

2. During the day

Dayspring

I don't think Thomas would have been welcomed by the other apostles. The Bible says he wasn't with the others when Jesus came (Jn 20:24). He was full of doubts about this Jesus that he had given his life to who was now dead and buried.

But Thomas came back to them. Maybe like the cousin who left, never kept in touch and then arrived home, he didn't get a great welcome. The other apostles only say to him, 'We have seen the Lord' (Jn 20:25). That's what they were telling everybody with excitement and joy.

And Thomas was a doubter. If you told him it was a fine day, he'd say, 'I think it's going to rain. A beautiful place, but it would be awful if it rained.' Thomas was like that.

He was having none of this faith. He said, 'Unless I see the mark of the nails in his hands and put my finger in the mark of the nails and my hand in his side, I will not believe.' Jesus said do that. Thomas didn't! There's nowhere in the gospel that says Thomas touched the wounds. His belief was on faith. Always called 'doubting Thomas', he should be known for changing his mind and believing.

He just said, 'My Lord and my God' (Jn 20:28), not my friend, not my master, but *my Lord and my God*.

All sorts of faith keep us going in life. We believe in God. We believe in love. We believe in those who guide our lives in family and state. Our deepest beliefs keep us going in life, and our belief in life after death grounds our acceptance of death.

We can see that for Thomas the Resurrection happened when he returned to the group. It happened in the ordinary, as it would happen for two disciples on the road to Emmaus and others at breakfast in Galilee.

We are part of the Resurrection when we have faith, when we forgive people, when we help each other. And when we pray, take part in the Eucharist, that's all taking part in the Resurrection. The Resurrection is not just for heaven. It is an ongoing feast, a part of our daily life. As the poet Gerard Manley Hopkins writes, 'Let him Easter in us, be a dayspring to the dimness of us'.

Something to think and pray about today
I can always change my mind and believe.

A word from the *Messenger*
'Perhaps we all have a touch of Old Testament logic in the recesses of our hearts: "You do the crime, you do the time" as prisoners admit. In doubting times my favourite quote on this great hope [of the Resurrection] comes from the first Eucharistic Prayer for Reconciliation: "You have bound the human race to yourself, with a love so tight that it can never be undone." This keeps me going in my faulty intercession for our world's salvation. Wayward we certainly are but still beloved: each of us a brother or sister for whom Christ died (Rm 8:11).' – Brian Grogan SJ, 'Pilgrims of Hope'

2. During the day

The Shelterers

At the Our Father of the Mass on a rainy Sunday, I could see a rush of people coming into the porch and into the church. It was the Sunday of an All-Ireland hurling final, and I thought they might be slipping in to offer a prayer for their county team, but then I realised it was to shelter from a downpour on their way to Croke Park. They sheltered, and they moved on when the shower was over. Mass continued.

Some of the people who come to church are like that. They seek shelter just for a few minutes. The shelterers are those who come to find some peace, silence and consolation at bad times. They may have sporadic attendance at Mass, but they come to pray or just to sit there and get something of what the Lord offers.

They come to pray for a loved one or to light a candle. They come to visit the crib at Christmas or the Easter garden. They come for a funeral. Why do many who hardly come near the church at any other time want the church at that time, either for themselves or someone else? They are seeking shelter from despair and from the downpours of life.

The church can be a space of peace and healing. Each person who comes to church comes with a hope, and these hopes must not be dashed by a lack of welcome or a superficial offering of spiritual comfort.

Today if you are coming to the church in search of shelter, I welcome you. And if someone comes to you today in search of a little shelter, I ask that you welcome them and offer them the spiritual comfort they need.

2. During the day

Something to think and pray about today
Each person who comes to church comes with a hope.

A word from the *Messenger*
'Aelred of Rievaulx wrote, "Here we are, you and I and, I hope, Christ the third in our midst." Dare I suggest that one of those fruits we can bring into being, or develop more fully, in ourselves is our capacity for true, loyal, reliable, kind and generous friendship? For the weary ones around us, we can become for them, with God's help, a sheltering tree and a true friend.' – Aideen Madden, 'Friendship', May 2017

2. During the day

Always the Better

At the funeral of a friend, everyone repeated to me, 'She had eighty-eight good years.' And she had, and many more had good years because of her! I knew her and the family for forty-two of those years. Widowed at thirty-eight, she brought up her three children on her own. She also helped rear the families of a brother and sister who both tragically died young. She was one of these people who seemed to receive more than her fair share of life's blows, but she was never overwhelmed by them. She loved her family but did not control them, and not only trusted them in their development but even got some fun out of the vagaries of their teenage years.

A quality she shared with any holy person I've met was a sense of humour. An evening in her house among her family was a fun time. Not even a disaster was without its moment of laughter, and no sorrow was without its memory of joy. I left her house always the better for it. Her faith was strong. She was a thoughtful, sincere and committed Catholic. She loved Mass and prayer but could be as annoyed as any with the drab liturgies we often 'celebrate'. Her year always included the nine days of the Novena of Grace. Her faith was not blind and was open to the goodness of God and the goodness of others. For her both were linked. She passed on a human sort of faith to her grandchildren, who held hands around the grave and said the prayer she had taught them, 'O Angel of God'.

In my time as a priest, I have met many like her who are an inspiration and encouragement to my priesthood. She had a brother who was a priest, so she knew well the shortcomings as well as the strengths of the priesthood. Her last words to me were 'Not long left, but I'm going to enjoy what I have.' She never pretended to be better or worse than she was, and she saw the good in everyone. Some people leave behind a memory larger than life.

Today can you think of someone who inspired and encouraged you? Maybe you can tell them how grateful you are for them.

Something to think and pray about today
The goodness of God and the goodness of others are linked.

A word from the *Messenger*
'The prophet Daniel has told us that "those who lead many to virtue will shine like the stars for all eternity" (Dn 12:3) – beautiful words of encouragement for us. How do we lead others to virtue? Surely it is by the example of our own lives. Many of us may be daunted by the very idea of leading others to virtue, but the oft-repeated words of Jesus – "Be not afraid" – must surely give us grace and courage.' – Aideen Madden, 'The Power of Good Example', February 2020

2. During the day

Church Bells

In Ireland people think of the Angelus when they think of church bells. At 6pm each day, before the evening news, RTÉ, the Irish broadcaster, plays a recording of the sound of the Angelus bells ringing for one minute.

Do you know what gives the church bell its joyful sound? Inside there is a tiny ball that strikes against the inside of the bell, producing a ringing sound. Without it there would be no sound!

Our joy comes from the inside too. It comes from having love for Jesus and for God in our hearts. The Bible says that even though we haven't seen Jesus, we believe in him and love him, and because of that love, we are filled with glorious joy. Into the very midst of life, God comes. We all know the story. God comes into a mother's womb, into a country under occupation, is born into a family, and is a migrant at birth. And it is still the same today: God is in the midst of all the life we have, good and bad.

If you hold your bell too tightly, it won't have a very joyful sound when you ring it. It's the same with our faith. Our hands have dampened the sound of the bells, and the ringing is no longer bright and joyful.

The Church can be a threatening place for some. People feel unwelcome, maybe even judged. But we come to Mass just as we are, just as the shepherds came to the crib: no tickets on the way in and no cross-examination. We are all welcome. The reason we are there is the universal love of God for all of us. When we realise that God's door is open to all, then the door of our heart opens too.

Pope Francis said, 'A Christian without joy is not a Christian.' Today, can we imagine the joy in our heart like the ball within the bell? What sound will it make as it strikes in us?

Something to think and pray about today
God is in the midst of my life.

A word from the *Messenger*
'God desires for us to live a joyful life. Not only occasionally, but continuously. Sustainable joy is, in other words, a sign of growing closeness to God. On the other hand, fear, emptiness, sadness or joy that turns into dryness after the experience that gave rise to it are rather a sign of the increasing separation from God or the traps of the evil one, the devil or, as Ignatius likes to call him, the enemy of human nature.' – Nikolaas Sintobin SJ, 'Ignatius 500', February 2022

2. During the day

Salt Shaker

In many ways, Jesus linked his teaching with examples of ordinary life. He talks about his followers being the salt of the earth and the light of the world (Mt 5:13–16). People would have been very familiar with salt in a time with few other flavourings, and light would have meant something different in a time without electricity.

I remember when we were told that salt was bad for us and the sprinkling of salt liberally over dinner stopped. The taste of the meal disimproved and many other limits followed. Then we went back to salt being okay, in moderation of course!

Jesus knew like ourselves the necessity for salt to keep food edible and to flavour it. He knew that carelessness meant that salt would lose its taste, being no good for anything.

Salt improves the taste and brings out the taste. The salt of the Gospel of Jesus fulfils our human life. The Gospel brings light on ordinary life so that we are the 'light of the world', not to be hidden. Jesuit author Teilhard de Chardin said that 'we are spiritual beings on a human journey'. The spirit-nature of our being is what lasts through life and into eternity. It brings hope, consolation, joy and perseverance to our lives. This is something of what Jesus means in his view of salt and light. We can be the bringers of peace, the cause of joy and the sureness of love in human life.

As salt can lose its flavour and goodness, so can our Christian life, which keeps its flavour by nourishing it with prayer, generosity and thought for others, both those nearby and far away.

Salt keeps food from being tasteless; our prayer and generosity and our reading of the Gospels keep our joy alive. Light gives us direction and our bearings; our Gospel keeps the light of God's joy shining.

We are called to be tasty salt and shining light for the world of today!

Something to think and pray about today
The salt of the Gospel of Jesus fulfils my human life.

A word from the *Messenger*
'The enlivening presence of mysticism – that of the "greats" and that of ordinary believers – is essential for the Church's well-being. Without it the Church loses its God-centredness, fails to witness effectively and lacks the inner fire needed for mission. It will soon be no more than a well-meaning NGO. The salt will have lost its taste; the light will be dimmed, if not extinguished.'
– Brian O'Leary SJ, *Ignatius Loyola: Christian Mystic* (2023)

Letters

Letters come into the offices of the *Messenger* from all parts of Ireland, North and South, and from Britain. The staff of the *Messenger* value these letters and ensure that they are placed at the altar of the Sacred Heart in the office chapel. Writing in petition and thanks is a way of praying. It is also a way of joining a community of praying people. Those who write in are remembered in prayer at the weekly Mass, even though I cannot respond to each.

Often letters come to the *Messenger* from people who live in areas where they have little chance of joining a faith community except for the Sunday Mass. Sharing prayers somehow makes them more immediate and real. They become expressions of faith within a community.

The letters that come to the *Messenger* are a kind of social history. They are about mortgages, marriages, addiction, court cases, driving tests, family members away from home, struggles with sexual identity and help with exams. Many letters give thanks for recovery from illnesses or ask for good results in medical tests. These letters are honest and from the heart, and they are based on a strong trust in God. The writers know that not everything will go their way in life, but they know that with God, things will go God's way. As I open these letters with their petitions and their thanks, I imagine God reading them. I know that God wants to give everyone what is best.

It is harder and harder to imagine people today taking the time to write a letter of petition or thanksgiving. More and more people find themselves isolated, and younger people in particular seem unable to reach out to friends and family not to mention to the *Messenger*!

Today take a moment to sit down and write a letter to God from the heart. What would you ask for? What would you be grateful for?

Something to think and pray about today
God wants to give everyone what is best.

A word from the *Messenger*
'All human life is there [in thanksgiving letters]. All human hopes and fears are there. Some are short, and some are long; some are elegantly written with full stops and capital letters in the right places, and some painfully lettered in pencil, barely literate and hardly legible. But God can read every sort of handwriting, just as he can read every heart.' – Paul O'Reilly SJ, 'Every Sort of Handwriting', August 2019

2. During the day

Waiting

Advent is the annual season of waiting. We wait for the same reason every year, and we are certain that the One we await – a person, Jesus, Son of God – will arrive on time. Yet, we find that the waiting is new each year, as Jesus is ever new. Maybe we don't like the waiting, or maybe we enter enthusiastically into Advent, which in some countries now starts in October. Maybe we are happy to wait in patience and quiet.

Some wait actively, reminding themselves each day with prayer or reflection as to why they wait. As Pope Francis says in *Let Us Dream*, our waiting is with the head (thinking about Advent), the heart (feeling with the season) and with the feet (doing something for others each day).

There's a richness in waiting. I find sometimes, and I'm impatient, that when I relax into waiting, something good happens for me. Whether it's waiting for a bus or a plane, or queueing in a shop, I notice different things about people or even new colours in the sky. I notice how I am in myself, and, like in waiting for sleep, I may make sense of the stresses of the day. Waiting in many ways is a good thing for us.

We wait also to notice where and how God is in our lives. This waiting is often compared to the watchman who waits, noticing all that is happening around. He's on a height to see the world around him. Each day we gather something new about God, ourselves and the world.

Today can you take notice of yourself in times of waiting? The way you wait may grow in you a new realisation that everything about God, and especially God's Son, is worth the waiting. Wait for the Lord, because his day is near. Thanks be to God!

Something to think and pray about today
There's a richness in waiting.

A word from the *Messenger*
'Waiting can be a crucible to refine our true self. As we wait on God, our hope needs to be in God's will and not in test results, doctors or even ourselves. In times of darkness and medical uncertainty, there has been a clarion call in my soul to reach for a higher consciousness and seek God's grace to intercede through the Holy Spirit to reveal a new way. This call prompts total trust from within, and my spiritual or intuitive guidance helps me navigate the uncertainty of the waiting process. There's a deep, inner urge to have faith and remain patient, knowing God has a plan.' – Andrea Hayes, 'Faithful Waiting', September 2023

2. During the day

Mr Hanley

As a young lad with a stutter, most teachers passed me by when time came to check if everyone had learned the week's lesson. That gave me a clear run at homework not done, but it made me feel different from everyone else. I felt bad about myself. Did my stutter mean I would be ignored, thought little of in life?

One teacher, Bill Hanly, whom I kept some contact with later, always asked me questions. He waited patiently until I got through it or quietly and gently asked, 'Did you learn this last night?' Though I was embarrassed by my disability, this made me feel I was one of the gang, ordinary. This memory remains with me always. There are lessons here on how to treat disability, illness or differences between people. Even though I was not mocked or given out to for my slowness in speech, when I was ignored I began to feel like a different sort of person. It's as if I was being hallmarked by my stutter. It was always there!

My stutter went, thank God, with some good speech training. Later in life, I became a teacher, and I tried to live out the lessons that Mr Hanly taught me. I tried to be kind to those in class who were different. Even though I did not always succeed, I learned to see the best in everyone. I trusted that the God who had helped me would in his own time help those in my care too.

Has there been a time in your life when you felt different? Could you take time to notice and help someone in a similar situation today? Maybe it is you who needs help? Trust that God helps, and look out for God in the form of the many Mr Hanleys of the world.

Something to think and pray about today
I trust that God will help me.

A word from the *Messenger*
'When we feel something deeply, it is good to share it with another person. Who better than God to share it with? So, we talk to God, as a person talks to a friend, letting him know how we feel, honestly, as he would want us to, then some silence. God may put something in our heart or mind. He communicates with us individually and personally, as a teacher does with a pupil.' – Kevin O'Rourke SJ, January 2019

2. During the day

Second Home

~~~

Ever wonder about the feast of the Presentation of the Lord? It is one of the principal feasts of the Church though often forgotten. The forty days after Christmas mark it as really important; all the forty-day periods of the Bible mark something important.

It was Jesus going home! His Temple would be a sort of home. It is more than visiting home; it is taking over the Temple as his home. 'A great prophet has arisen among us! ... God has visited his people!' (Lk 7:16–17). The different parts of Simeon's prayer welcome Jesus into his home – not that he will always be received well there.

The Temple was the place of God and God's presence for his people. It housed the Ark of the Covenant, a sign of God's continual presence.

A look from the hilltop near where I live shows about twenty spires: churches of different denominations that bring us to our memories of God. I can see where I was baptised, where friends were married and even – wait for it – where I will be buried!

These were homes of God for us, places where we often went for the forgiveness of our sins and for the big occasions of life – birth and marriage. In fact they are second homes for us.

Today, could you visit your second home? Maybe pick out the church spire from the skyline and head there?

Many a parent brings the child to the church, as Mary and Jospeh did with Jesus; it would be lovely ceremony to bring back – the blessing of children.

Mary and Joseph brought Jesus to the Temple, and later they would find him there, where he would learn about God and fulfil some of his mission.

If you cannot get out today, you can remember that the Temple now is not to be just a building; it is where we find God: in nature, in truth and above all in each other. You are a temple of the Holy Spirit.

Something to think and pray about today
The Church is a second home for me.

A word from the *Messenger*
'The landscape and community to which human living is adapted by nature and evolution equate broadly in terms of scale with the landscape units that were adopted as parishes by the early Church. Think of it as the cultural counterpart to the ecosystem, but much broader and richer because of the cultural embroidery we lay over it. The word 'parish' comes from the Latin *paroecia*, which is the Greek *paroikía*: the area around my home. Interestingly there is no such word in classical Latin; it only came into use with Christianity.' – John Feehan, 'Rediscovering the Parish', March 2025

2. During the day

Pointing North

As St Ignatius of Loyola was about to leave Jerusalem in 1523, he made a secret trip to a place associated with the Ascension of the Lord on the Mount of Olives. He wanted to find out whether the feet of Jesus were pointing north or south! For years I thought this was a pious concern. Why would it matter? The tradition Ignatius was following claimed that if the feet pointed southwards, the followers of Jesus were directed southwards to proclaim the Gospel only among the Jewish people. If they were facing northwards, it would mean the Gospel was intended for the whole world.

At the time of Ignatius, this place was in the hands of the Ottoman Empire. Ignatius had to bribe a guard with a pair of scissors to gain entry! Pilgrims still visit this site today, and it is venerated by Christians and Muslims alike. You can read more about it in Josef Briffa SJ's excellent guide, *Ignatius in the Holy Land* (Messenger Publications, 2023).

Ignatius found that the feet pointed to the north. Did this visit contribute to the future world vision of Ignatius? His new Society of Jesus would go to the ends of the then-known world to spread the gospel message. The countries of the East – India and Japan – were lands of mystery and of exotic silks, foods and scents. For Ignatius, they were lands ready to hear the Gospel of Jesus Christ.

From 1540–1556, Ignatius lived in a small house in Rome, never travelling again. His world-view, however, was global. While he said goodbye to travel, he did not say goodbye to the wider world. His wider world was in living each day intensely. He wrote letters to Jesuits abroad, administered the new Society and linked his daily work with contemplation of the heavens in prayer.

2. During the day

The Ascension signifies the end of Jesus' earthly life and the introduction of the Gospel to the world – to be shared through the lives of his followers. In leaving a specific earthly place, Jesus was available to the world. I was wrong. There is a big lesson to be learned from Jesus' feet pointing northwards. Jesus' followers are to go to the periphery, to those places of need in society and the world, places no one else will go. This periphery can be far flung, as it was for St Francis Xavier, who travelled to India and Japan; but it can also be reached from your desk, if you follow Ignatius's example of living each day with deliberation.

In accounts of the Ascension, the disciples are 'sent back' to the city, to ordinary homelessness and hardship, ordinary joy and sorrow. The Lord of heaven and earth is present everywhere.

Something to think and pray about today
Which way do my feet point today?

A word from the *Messenger*
'There is a little ritual, now no longer part of the liturgy, whereby the priest, after reading the gospel on Ascension Thursday, blows out the Paschal Candle. This ritual symbolises that going forward Jesus, who over forty days appeared to the disciples and was seen visibly through their human eyes, would only be visible through the eyes of faith, something which only the Holy Spirit makes possible.' – Shane Daly SJ, 'Pentecost', May 2023

2. During the day

Trust

~~~~~~

Colm Brophy recounted an insight from a child about God in an issue of the *Messenger*:

> 'I'm drawing a picture of God,' Aoife said confidently. 'But Aoife,' replied the teacher, 'you know that God is very special. God is someone you cannot see. We don't know what God looks like.' 'Well,' said Aoife, 'when I'm finished this picture you'll know what God looks like.'

The smallest of our children can say and ask things that have a serious side to them: Why is the weather different each day? Where did granddad go when he died?

Many situations in life we take on trust. We trust one another, ourselves and our leaders. In the small and big things, we have trust.

What about faith? The centre of faith is trust. The trust of faith is trusting in God, whatever we think of God or believe God to be. We don't know much about God. It's often said, following St Augustine, that everything we say about God is wrong. We don't know the full truth. The words we use are human words. Take love for example. When we talk of God as love, it's a different form of love in many ways to the human. God's love is totally unconditional, forgiving and for everyone.

Today remember that faith is a journey not a destination. We are sometimes not confident that we are on the right road. Love is a journey, as is any commitment or decision in life. The task of faith in life is to believe what we cannot see. The reward of faith will be to see what we have believed in. These are the two big 'trusts' of our lives.

Maybe we can only grasp these truths of faith with the eyes of faith, as they say. In the present, however, we 'see' God in the ways people live out lives of love and faith around us.

Something to think and pray about today
We don't know the full truth.

A word from the *Messenger*
'Great advances in scientific knowledge, particularly in cosmology and quantum physics, give room for our imaginations to wander and wonder, just as we do when we ponder on the beauty of our planet. We can create an image, like the five-year-old Aoife did, that visually tries to embody an invisible truth.' – Colm Brophy, 'Seeing the Invisible', September 2022

2. During the day

Eternity Today

The Resurrection is the mystery our Christian faith is based on. Paul writes, 'if Christ has not been raised, then our proclamation is in vain and your faith is in vain' (1 Cor 15:14). In the words of a poster slogan: 'We are Easter people, and "Alleluia" is our song.'

We live in the atmosphere or the ecosystem of eternity, where the Lord dwells. In the risen Lord, earth and heaven meet. The Sufi writer Kahlil Gibran, among his many writings on eternity, says, 'In the depths of your hopes and desires, lies your silent knowledge of the beyond, and like seeds dreaming beneath the snow, your heart dreams of spring. Trust the dreams, for in them is hidden the gate to eternity.'

Eternity, the life of heaven, is not just for heaven. Jesus came 'to give life and give it to the full' (Jn 10:10) here and now, today. This divine life is also quite ordinary. Resurrection is known and appreciated in the flowering of the seed, the growth of a tree, the incoming tide – all ways in which the love and power of God is evident. Creation is a gift of the risen Lord, for 'nothing has come into being except through him' (Jn 1:3). Gerard Manley Hopkins puts this well in his poem 'Easter':

> Gather gladness from the skies;
> Take a lesson from the ground;
> Flowers do open their heavenward eyes
> And a Spring-time joy have found;
> Earth throws Winter's robes away,
> Decks herself for Easter Day.

Predominant in the climax of God's creation are men and women created in love. In the love of each other, the forgiveness of each other and the ways we bring life – physical and spiritual – to each other, we share in the life of the risen Lord. We are ministers of the Resurrection to each other, sharing Gibran's link of heaven and earth, so that all life is a breath of resurrection.

Something to think and pray about today
The life of heaven is not just for heaven.

A word from the *Messenger*
"'He who carries God in his heart bears heaven with him wherever he goes,' says St Ignatius of Loyola. For him offering everything to the creator in gratitude is prayer. He prayed to give everything: 'Take, O Lord, and receive my entire liberty, my memory, my understanding and my whole will. All that I am and all that I possess you have given me. I surrender it all to you to be disposed of according to your will. Give me only your love and your grace; with these I will be rich enough, and will desire nothing more.'" – Sunny Jacob SJ, 'Growing in Prayer and Faith', June 2022

2. During the day

Down to Earth

As I was walking up the corridor after what I thought was a good homily, a 'Dub' lady said to me, 'Ah for God's sake Father, come down to earth!'

I often think on the feast of the Assumption of Mary that she could get the same comment! The first reading of the feast has the image of Mary with twelve stars around her head, shining bright. 'Come down to earth!'

Then we get to the gospel, which does bring us down to earth. It's the story of Mary going to help her cousin Elizabeth, an older lady who is also pregnant. Like any expectant mother, Elizabeth needs companionship, ordinary love, someone to share the problems and joys with. It is because Mary is like that, in helping Elizabeth and later in bringing up and supporting Jesus, that she is now in glory. We could say of Mary she did ordinary things extraordinarily well. The visit to Elizabeth is one of these ordinary things done in love and care.

There are many little visitations in life: to be present with people when they need us; visiting when we can; looking out for people who are housebound and a bit afraid to go out or use public transport or afraid of people for their safety; helping parents prepare children maybe for their first day at school; accompaniment at bereavement or illness. Support and care in difficult times together.

Can you visit someone today who needs your support and care? In doing that, like Mary, you bring the grace of God and the presence of the Lord. When you think of Jesus' words 'just as you did it to one of the least of mine, you did it to me' (Mt 25:40), you can think of Mary.

The feast of the Assumption is not just about the heavenly life of Mary but about her engagement with you now in your life, a mother and friend in heaven.

Something to think and pray about today
Mary did ordinary things extraordinarily well.

A word from the *Messenger*
'If Mary's life shows us the shape of our own faith journey, the Assumption shows us our final destiny. The feast of her Assumption celebrates her full sharing in the risen life of Christ. As one who now shares fully in the Lord's risen life, we can confidently turn to her, asking her to pray for us now so that we can be the complete disciple of the Lord that she was and to pray for us at the hour of our death so that we too can come to share in the Lord's risen life to the full.' – Martin Hogan, 'The Assumption of Mary', August 2023

2. During the day

Young and Old

When I was young, I used to ask my grandmother how old my mother was all the time. I was told that ladies never tell their age. My mother and grandmother came from a time when a woman never told her age. When I couldn't get an answer from my grandmother, I used to go and ask my grandfather the same question! He would just reply that his memory was bad, and he couldn't remember things like that. One day I stopped asking because I found my mother's passport!

When you ask the right questions, grandparents have memory and wisdom to share. If you are young, you might ask an elder today about hard times in life, their faith or just how they are doing. If you are older, you might reach out to a youngster today and encourage them to meet times of growth and difficulty with love and acceptance. Young people today need encouragement to pray, to do good in their lives and to care for their neighbour.

Society often belittles the elderly, demanding they downsize their lives, cutting their social welfare and failing to provide them with good medical care. This leads to feelings of isolation. Young people too feel isolated by the pressures and false expectations of a materialist culture. Ironically, this shared isolation goes unnoticed, and just as the young feel misunderstood by the old, the old feel misunderstood by the young.

It's said that 'an ounce of encouragement is worth a ton of exhortation'. Everyone needs the touch of affirmation, gratitude and hope. The old have much to be grateful for, and the young have much to hope for. Whether you are young or old, today share what you have, receive what you don't and be that touch of affirmation for one another.

Something to think and pray about today
Everyone needs the touch of affirmation, gratitude and hope.

A word from the *Messenger*
'I remember once a child asking me if the trees whisper to each other in a forest. But trees also comingle their roots in the darkness underground, just as the islands plunge together into the mother-seas of our expansive oceans. Differences and boundaries are but accidental fences in the eternal continuum of God's grace. We are both a forest and a single tree that unites the *older* past with the *elder* promise of a new growth that is caressed by the invisible breath and breeze of God.' – Fr John Cullen, 'Elder versus Older', September 2024

3: At night

Prayer at Night

I am thankful for the times today when I heard your voice, Lord.
Forgive me Lord for when I heard your voice but did not act, and instead turned away from you.
Tomorrow, may I let you into my life,
and may I be an apostle sent from your heart to the heart of the world.
Amen.

As the sun sets at the close of the day,
I consider the many moments of the day.
I recognise the good and the bad.
I offer everything to you and to your mercy, Lord.
Help me to grow more and more in my capacity to love others as you love them.
Amen.

3. At night

I still myself and breathe deeply.
I call to mind one thing that I am thankful for.
I call to mind one act of love or kindness or compassion that I witnessed today.
I call to mind one thought or action of mine of love or selflessness.
I call to mind one action of mine today of selfishness.
I know that I am forgiven.
I breathe deeply and am thankful for the day.
Amen.

Father, as I prepare for sleep tonight,
let me know the warmth of your love.
In your mercy, soothe my pain,
whether in my body, mind or soul.
Grant me a restful night of sleep so that when I awake,
I'm strengthened to do your will.
Amen.

3. At night

My thanks for the good of this day,
the good done for me and the good I did.
I ask you to help those I met today who needed help,
and forgive any wrong I have done.
Give to me and all I think of now the peace of a restful night,
so I may be ready for love and service tomorrow.
Amen.

Dear Lord, the evening comes, the day is done.
Let peace wash over my household
throughout the dark of night and in the few still hours of the morning.
Wipe away my troubles.
Cleanse me of worry and doubt.
May your magnificent good be my protection for evermore.
Amen.

3. At night

Returning Home

You might remember being told as a kid to come back home in time for bed. I remember I didn't always want to come back! I was out with pals. In later life, I was happy to come home. It was where I belonged. When I drive through the places I lived years ago, I am reminded that home is always home.

Somebody was asked once 'Why do you bother staying in the Church?' The answer: 'I've no other spiritual home.' We'll hear the Word and return. We stray away from God in small journeys and big ones. We might not feel like returning, but when we do, we know we're home. Why?

Church is home because it is where Jesus lives – not in the building only but in the people. Jesus lives with each of us, as he makes his home with us. He lives also among us in community, as wherever two or three are gathered in his name (Mt 18:20), he is with us.

Something to think and pray about tonight
Hear the Word and return.

A word from the *Messenger*
'Home is not necessarily a geographical place but a personal centre, or what Scripture calls "the heart". This home is our own creation through experience, choice and habit. This is the home and location that Jesus invites us to make of his Word.' – Fr Alan Hilliard, 'Stay at Home', July 2022

3. At night

Dread of Tomorrow

I generally liked August – until the end of the month. Our family sometimes had a short holiday in the West of Ireland in the first half of the month, and then there would be the buying of the school uniform and new or second-hand books – bought in Pembreys bargain shop – in the second. We knew then that the dreaded date of returning to school was near.

Like a lot of things dreaded, it was not as bad as I expected. It was good to meet new people, and my teachers were not so bad. Sport would begin with hopes of winning the cup later in the year, and the school clubs, like the camera club, would get going again, and I could suffer through the most boring classes.

That's the way mostly – all of our lives are a mixture of what we like and love, dislike and dread. Parents love their children and maybe dread the day they will leave home; the life the children and their friends brought to the house is gone, and the silence for a while is oppressive. We can let the dread overcome us, so that we fear the future so much that we can't enjoy the present, like the person who always says on a fine day at the beach, 'This would be an awful place in the rain.'

'Weeping may linger for the night, but joy comes with the morning' (Ps 30:5). We allow ourselves to really believe and trust in the light of life in the middle of the darkness.

Jesus was like that – he never spoke of his death without mention of the Resurrection. For him there was always light in the darkness. This is one of his gifts to all of us, coming from his love. His hope for us is that we would find the light in bad times and know that he himself is with us all our days.

3. At night

Something to think and pray about tonight
I allow myself to believe and trust in the light of life in the middle of the darkness.

A word from the *Messenger*
'I think of Jesus' words to Peter when he told him he would give him the keys to the kingdom of heaven. Without the key, the only way to gain entrance to anything is through breaking in, and, if we break in, we are always trespassers. When we have the key, the door is ours to open. What is this key? Where do we find it? Who gives it to us? The key is mercy. We find it in the living of life and in moments we encounter, where we have received mercy from another or found, within ourselves, the ability to be merciful to another. God, through his Word and presence in our lives, is the giver of the key.' – Fr Vincent Sherlock, 'Taking the Key', July 2024

3. At night

Walk a Mile in My Moccasins

He was an entertaining man, full of stories and reminiscences and a great talker. He was a man known for his witty but rather judgemental comments about others. One evening he was in high flight, telling me all about a mutual friend's flaws. He calmed down and tempered his judgement when I told him, 'Funny, I met Seamus last week, and he had nothing but praise for you!'

We are all prone to judging others. We give out about them, and we gossip about them. We even judge entire groups of people who are unlike us in age, belief or appearance. It's human to do so, but it is harmful. Jesus was a man of few personal judgements. He didn't judge even those who let him down. To a woman being harshly judged, he said I do not condemn you (Jn 8:11). To Peter, who had denied him, he just asked for love. To all of us he says, do not judge and you will not be judged.

Tonight as you reflect on the day, think of someone you may have judged or gossiped about. Pause and reflect on their good points, of what you are grateful for in them. Look at yourself and find out why you were harsh. Often what you judge in another, you dislike in yourself. You can pray for a person who may have harmed you. Small things get you out of this judging mode.

There is a Native American saying: 'You don't know another until you have walked in his moccasins.' There is so much about you that is hidden to others, and even hidden to you! Remember that you share the dignity of being a child of God with others, your brothers and sisters in Christ. You may find that when you become less harsh and judgemental of others, you are happier in yourself.

3. At night

Something to think and pray about tonight
Jesus didn't judge those who let him down.

A word from the *Messenger*
'We can be judgemental, shutting our eyes and ears to the poor while welcoming the rich. When we make distinctions among ourselves, we close ourselves to the gift that each person is.' – Fr Tom Cox, 'Selective Listening', November 2018

3. At night

A Few Hours' Camino

When Pope Francis visited Ireland in 2018, I decided to walk from Leeson Street to the papal Mass in Dublin's Phoenix Park. I took it as a kind of pilgrimage – a few hours' Camino. As I walked, I began to wonder why people go on pilgrimage. I think they want to learn what they believe, as Guy Stagg puts it in *The Crossway*. I found myself asking, 'What do I believe in my heart?'

I came up with a few answers. I love the Church with all its faults. I believe in looking to the peripheries, looking homelessness and poverty in the eye. I value my relationship with Our Lady. Prayer is important to me. I believe that one day I will see God.

Tonight, as you reflect on the day, can you give a bit of time to learning what you believe? It's a different thing to believing what you have learned!

When I look over crowded churches at Christmas, I see all sorts of people. What I call the regulars, the occasionals and the annuals! I wonder if people ever stop and ask themselves why they go to Mass at Christmas. If they did, they might discover something about what they really believe in.

Life is a bit like that. You might find yourself being extra kind to a stranger. And so you find that you believe in kindness! A pilgrimage ends with what you bring home. What did you bring home today?

3. At night

Something to think and pray about tonight
What do I believe in my heart?

A word from the *Messenger*
'I wonder why we are so driven and focused on ourselves in our society. The normality of this makes it so challenging to recognise the needs of others sometimes. One thing I noticed about all of the people I met on the Camino is that they have a glow of happiness about them, a joy and easiness which is contagious. Is it service to others and to the Lord that makes them happy?' – Eoghan Keogh, 'The Spirit of the Camino', August 2017

3. At night

No-vember

A Jesuit friend of mine, now deceased, used to announce every 1 November, 'No light, no heat, no warmth, No-vember!'

Life can feel like that sometimes. You find yourself in a wintry time of life. The nights are long, and the days tough. But just as there is no winter that does not go into summer, there is no darkness in life that does not have its promise and its goodness. You can find hope, consolation and joy in the worst of times. Many a tragedy brings out the best in people.

Jesus said, 'Come to me, all you who are weary and are carrying heavy burdens, and I will give you rest' (Mt 11:28–30). This care promised by Jesus is often brought by others. They are points of light in the winter of life. While human friendship and support do not take away the darkness and sadness, they do bring the light.

In churches up and down the country you can find the light of prayer shining, an atmosphere of the Resurrection. It is warmth in winters of death and loss. It is the promise of Jesus who is the Resurrection and the Life.

Tonight ask yourself where you might find the care promised by Jesus. Could it be in the listening presence of a friend or in a visit to your church? Jesus brings that care to you through others, and in times of winter they are a light that shines in the darkness and is not overcome by it (Jn 1:5).

Something to think and pray about tonight
I can find hope, consolation and joy even in the worst of times.

A word from the *Messenger*
'Back in Tennessee, in 30°C heat, I saw a man with a cowboy hat standing in the traffic holding a sign saying "Trust Jesus." That simple display reminded me of how private and simple was the faith of those who encouraged me.' – Elaine O'Sullivan, 'Meandering Journey', April 2020

3. At night

Saying Goodbye

After my brother's death, I went on a last visit to the family home. He had lived there since we first moved there in 1962. There was luck in getting the house and that the sale of the pub meant we could afford it.

Saying goodbye is often a wrenching experience. I hadn't lived there long, so it wasn't as difficult as it might have been. On that last visit, I realised that I was saying goodbye to the *house* and not the home. The home made in that house will always be a lively part of my life, with its memories and links to those gone before.

Some items in particular brought back the memories: a photo from the wall, an icon I gave my family, the last family photo we took, some other souvenirs brought to my parents when as children we started travelling, and the Sacred Heart.

What builds a home? Home is where a room is always there for us. It is a centre of warmth and upbringing and much more. It remains in the heart and thus does not always need a house, even though it began in a house. It is the focus of much reminiscence in the family. It is the centre from which we made friends among neighbours, some of whom we shared the avenue with for a long time. The people of our home and many neighbours live in our heart and memory forever.

With thanks I remembered that I grew up in the days before a mortgage, and a legacy from my grandfather to my father bought a good house then for €1000. In 1962 a move got us a lovely house for €4000. I grew up in the time when a house and its debt wasn't so much a worry. Do we not owe the new generation the same?

3. At night

Something to think and pray about tonight
My home remains in my heart.

A word from the *Messenger*
'We named our son after my father, because we wanted him to know where he came from and we wanted him to grow up knowing deep in his bones what we hoped for him: that he would come to have the character of his grandfather and live a life marked by faithfulness, gentleness and an eagerness to have fun and laugh. It is a matter of fact that my parents' generation could buy their houses easier and often could have one spouse stay at home. They had it hard too, however, in their own ways. I am deeply grateful that they are around to share their wisdom.' – Kevin Hargaden, 'Wisdom of All Ages', January 2019

3. At night

Remembering These Things Too

During the months of the Covid-19 pandemic, I got accustomed to watching Mass streamed on television. I watched it alone or even took part in it with the small Jesuit community at Leeson Street in Dublin, where I was living. I wondered, 'What's missing?', and I knew: people of course. The empty buildings RTÉ brought to my screen were always beautiful, but it's the people that make the Church. I missed Masses with people, the baptisms and even, as we say in Ireland, a decent funeral.

In fact I wonder what I missed most about not being able to go to Mass. Was it the Mass or the sense of community? I think it was both, taken together. The 10 am Mass in parishes is a community. It is sometimes light-heartedly called the 'grey-haired Mass'. It is often made up of those who live alone or who are searching for a sense of community. A parishioner once said to me, 'I look down from the gallery, and it's fifty shades of grey or fifty bald heads!' Grey is beautiful! And baldness too!

During the pandemic, we learned that we can be Church without a building. We can be Church in the home, as families watched Mass together and prayed together, and on the street, as priests and bishops blessed neighbourhoods and as people lined the streets in social distance for a funeral.

It's when we think of the people and their faith that we stop worrying too much about the future of the Church. Pope Francis said, 'Thinking of people anoints me, it does me good, it takes me out of my self-preoccupation' (interview with Austen Ivereigh in *Commonweal*). This is the faith that rolls around among us every time we meet, whether in a church, a sitting room or a kitchen.

During the pandemic, I wondered about all those I once

served. How were they doing? I missed them all: the one who looked totally bored during the homily; the one who lit candles during the consecration, with pennies clattering to the ground; the one who praised me profusely, and the one who criticised me! It's the people I missed the most.

Pope Francis quotes the poet Virgil: 'Perhaps one day it will be good to remember these things too.' Maybe the different Churches of different times – the Church of Covid-19 or the Church during times of persecution – remind us of who we really are as Church; we are those united in discipleship, community and the friendship of Jesus Christ.

Tonight, as you look back over the day, could you say the same? Maybe today was difficult, but perhaps one day it will be good to remember it too.

Something to think and pray about tonight
Church is wherever I am united with others in discipleship, community and the friendship of Jesus.

A word from the *Messenger*
'Spirituality is about awareness of reality and adjustment to it, acceptance of limitations and exploring of potential. As Pope Francis says, "God is in the real, not the ideal." This means finding God in the messiness and challenge of situations, finding a way through. We are limited and vulnerable but also have tremendous potential and hidden depths.' – Brendan McManus SJ, 'Gear Change', October 2024

3. At night

Follow the Light

An October afternoon hiking in the Comeragh Mountains started well for myself and a friend. So that we wouldn't get lost, I made note of some piles of newly-chopped wood on our way. We could use these 'landmarks' to guide us home.

The conversation flowed well and dusk fell without us noticing. It was time to go back. As we retraced our steps, we noticed that there were blocks of wood every hundred yards or so. Finding our path down the mountain would be next to impossible! Panic set in, and we feared being stranded in the wintry weather. What to do? Looking down from where we were, we could see the lights of cars. If we could head in that direction, we might get to safety. Taking a risk, we slowly went through the woods in a straight line, keeping an eye on the moving lights, our guide and security. Carefully we picked our way through branches and trees, with some limited conversation and a few prayers. Eventually we reached a road and looked for the car. We realised then that we were on the other side of the mountain! But at least we were on firm ground.

We headed for the nearest house, found a farmer and explained our predicament. Where were we? Where would we find the car? He pointed to his car and simply said, 'I do this run regularly.' We agreed with him that people should be better prepared for mountain walks in the late afternoon. He kindly drove us the six miles to the carpark. The lights had guided us, and the kindness of a stranger had brought us to safety. My friend, who always thought of himself as an expert mountain guide, doesn't like to remember this story, but it's the story of life.

Jesus calls himself 'the light of the world'. His light is your guide, but not your only guide. Other people cooperate with him in sharing the light of care, helpfulness and compassion with you; and you cooperate with him in doing the same for others.

Jesus lights your way, like those cars in the distance, but he also looks to you, in your own way, to carry his lamp.

Something to think and pray about tonight
Who shared the light of Jesus with me today?

A word from the *Messenger*
'The disciples are the light of the world. Light has already been mentioned as a metaphor for Christ and/or the preaching of the Gospel in Matthew 4:16. Elsewhere in Scripture, God is light (1 Jn 1:5; Ex 13:21; Ps 36:90). Light is also a biblical symbol for truth, knowledge and purity. "The entrance of your word gives light!" (Ps 119:130). After Pentecost the disciples will bring light to the world by preaching the Gospel, but here Jesus' emphasis is on the disciples' actions: "Just so, your light must shine before others, that they may see your good deeds and glorify your heavenly Father" (Mt 5:16).' – David Breen, 'Salt of the Earth and Light of the World', February 2023

3. At night

Come Rain or Shine

William Cowper once said, 'But it is a sort of April-weather life that we lead in this world. A little sunshine is generally the prelude to a storm.' Shakespeare wrote, 'April has put a spirit of youth in everything.' Consider that old country saying: 'April weather, rain and sunshine both together.'

In our faith life all this can ring true. So much in life can change so quickly. In the dark times, we wonder what it is that will last and what we can really do without.

Today is ending, but our faith is about what lasts forever. 'The Lord has risen indeed' (Lk 24:24), the followers of Jesus proclaimed to each other. Nothing can take this away. Even in Jesus' life, everything else passed – his childhood, adolescence, mission and death. But the life he has now with God and with us cannot be taken from him.

Neither can this risen life be taken from us. It is at the root of our faith, our worship and our hope. It gives us the sure and certain hope of sharing now and in eternity the risen life of the Lord.

3. At night

Something to pray and think about tonight
My life with Jesus lasts forever.

A word from the *Messenger*
'Our faith is both ancient and new. Christians of every time and place have placed their trust in the same loving, healing, saving Lord. Christ is the same yesterday, today and forever. It is our understanding of the faith that grows as our friendship with Christ matures. Every generation asks new questions, discovers new ways of communicating old truths and lives the one Gospel in new ways.' – Fr Albert McDonnell, 'The People of God on the Move', November 2023

3. At night

Lasting Self-Love

A young man in his late twenties enjoyed buying clothes. He was by no means wealthy, so he bought in bargain shops. Wanting to appear better, he would transfer the clothes to a designer shopping bag and go home with that. He even joked about it – a way of boasting or living up to appearances. Somehow the label gave him a lift about himself and how he might be seen by others. A sort of living up to society's expectations.

Everyone has a drive to feel good about themselves. It's just that today, people look in all the wrong places. They look at where they live or how educated they are, and some people even look down on others for the colour of their skin or for their religion. These things do not give a lasting self-love.

If you want to have a good image of yourself, you need a few things: acceptance of your good qualities and your gifts; the love of others who accept you as you are; a realistic view of your faults and failings; the grace to forgive yourself; some success in life.

There is also a self-love that comes from your faith. If God loves you unconditionally, and Jesus died and rose for you, why should you love yourself less? You are precious in the eyes of God and carved in love on the palm of God's hand.

Prayer can help with self-esteem. In prayer you can thank God for something good in your life. As you reflect on the day, even if it was a hard one, try and find one good thing to be grateful for and then, if you can, another.

3. At night

Something to think and pray about tonight
I am precious in the eyes of God.

A word from the *Messenger*
'The person with an appreciative heart approaches life in a different way. They appreciate that all they are has been given to them as a gift from somebody or something beyond themselves. As a result, they want to seek the giver of the gift to express gratitude. They know happiness is something they have to work for. They seek the values that offer the greatest opportunity of happiness for the greatest number. They sense they are being invited by the creator of all to steward all that exists according to the mind of the creator. They know they fail in this and that they fail to be loving a lot of the time. This saddens them but does not depress them. They are quick to say sorry, to learn from their mistakes and to try again to be who they sense they can be.' – Joe Hayes SJ, 'An Appreciative Heart', April 2025

3. At night

Everything Has Its Time

Some endings are unexpected, others are a long time coming. We have our memories of those gone before us. We have a treasure of good memories of loving family members and maybe some painful memories of separation and reconciliation; there are memories of school, the neighbourhood and countless small kindnesses.

Our faith helps with those painful memories of others, whether we miss them or regret some part of our relationship with them. They are now with God and the fullness of love, with maybe repentance for faults, sins and failings. With God we will be at our best in eternity.

At a time of endings, we can look back and see that many unexpected things in life were well worthwhile and brought us happiness, even if they were difficult at the time.

Tonight we pray for those who have gone before us.

A popular reading at a time of death is the 'Everything Has Its Time' reading from Ecclesiastes (1–9). The time of death is not of our choosing. It's not that God has the date of our death planned, rather it is that our body has its own clock and can last only so long. At that time God is very near, to welcome us home.

A favourite gospel of mine is the one where Jesus says, 'Do not let your hearts be troubled. Believe in God; believe also in me. In my Father's house there are many dwelling places. If it were not so, would I have told you that I go to prepare a place for you?' (Jn 14:1–2).

The funeral liturgy remembers with thanks a person's life but also faces the question 'Where are they now?' All we can say is that we will see God face to face and, in some mysterious way, be united with all those we knew and loved on earth.

Something to think and pray about tonight
With God I will be at my best in eternity.

A word from the *Messenger*
'Zacchaeus climbs a sycamore tree, a tree that grows very tall. He wants to see without being seen and to know more while remaining hidden. But the tree is not a hiding place. He is caught in the act! The tree is the place where he may be exposed to public shame and ridicule. But the opposite happens. Jesus honours and calls him by name: "Zacchaeus, hurry and come down. I must stay at your house today" (Lk 19:5). Imagine those words addressed to you. Jesus enters your home or homelessness. He has chosen to be your guest. He visits the familiar places of your life. He does it with grace and not judgement. He visits the hidden places of sadness, loss, shame, failure, sin and rejection. He sees your flaws and failures. He also sees your eternal life in the wounds – your own resurrection.' – Fr John Cullen, 'The Guest House', May 2025

3. At night

Images

It is often said of a new baby, 'He's the image of his dad' or 'She's the image of her granny.' This way links are made between the generations. Sometimes you see someone on the street and are reminded of someone you've not seen in a long time. For some 'people watching' is a pastime, and they watch others and wonder what they're like.

'Image' is a big word in the Bible. We are created in the image of God (Gn 1). Jesus is referred to as 'the image of the invisible God' (Col 1:15). When you look at Jesus or read of him or relate to him, you are in touch with God. 'Image' for the gospel writers does not mean something like a picture. It is your constant creation by God, as you are invited to be more like God.

You may be the image of your father or mother, but you have your own personality and uniqueness. In the same way, while you are in God's image, you are still unique. Each person is an image of something in God, for something of God lives in each person. God is as wide as the universe and all creation, and so being in God's image does not mean being slavishly like God or others, with nothing of your own.

You can be the image of God in your compassion and tenderness to others, your daily love for those close to you and for the poor. Loving people is the truest image of God. You are like Jesus not because you look or talk like him but because you live like him.

When I walk along the street sometimes, I look at people and think, 'She's the image of someone I know.' But of absolutely everyone I see, I can say that he or she is the image of God.

Tonight think back on the people you saw today. Each one was an image of God. What a thought!

3. At night

Something to think and pray about tonight
Each person I met today is an image of something in God.

A word from the *Messenger*
'What is salvation? It is perceived in varied manner. It has been made to seem unreal. In fact, salvation means nothing other than attaining perfect humanness. We are human beings, created in the image of God. Our destiny is to be fully human, as God understands humanness. This is the goal. When I am, at last, wholly what I am meant to be, I will have reached the goal; I will be wholly myself. But, here and now I am far short of what I am meant to be. What I must understand is that my ultimate salvation is God's achievement. God achieves our salvation through his Son, Jesus Christ.' – Wilfrid Harrington OP, 'Salvation', November 2019

3. At night

Letting Go

~~~

Some simple childhood memories last. One of mine is of my father teaching me to ride a bike. On the road we went, and he guided the bike, gently pushing. I felt very safe and confident with him pushing the bike. It was a good feeling, but after a while I realised I was cycling on my own. Without saying anything, he let me go, knowing that he had done his bit!

Parents tell us it is like that. Children are taught and guided, things done for them, advice taken and so on. The day comes of letting go. A parent told me of his fear as his son went off in the family boat for the first time without him. He knew that day had to come some time. The 'boy' became an expert sailor, bringing many an adult out for an afternoon on the boat.

Much of life is letting go – of roles in the family, jobs, family members who move out, friendships that fade and finally the letting go of death. Even going to bed is letting go of the day.

It can be really difficult to let go. A mother said, 'I really missed my son when he moved out, but, to be honest, I wasn't able to manage him much longer. It was time to let go into another sort of motherhood relationship with him.'

God is near at every letting go, as Mary found out when she waved goodbye to Jesus as he began his ministry, when her husband died, as she let go of her Son on Calvary, and finally in her death. At moments of letting go, God is near. He let his Son go when others needed him. In times of letting go, let God in! God is the one we need never let go, and the one who will never let go of any of us.

Something to think and pray about tonight
God is near at every letting go.

A word from the *Messenger*
'During the months of autumn, I am constantly reminded to be not afraid to delve into the barren edges of my own heart where feelings of loss and heartache hide in the shadows. These spaces are sometimes hidden out of fear or even shame. Yet autumn for me is the season of surrender, helping me to embrace a deeper understanding of myself and also a deeper spiritual intimacy with creation. God wants to be close to us, especially when we are afraid or struggling. If we look at the trees, their leaves are dying, but notice how they still stand tall and perfectly demonstrate what it means to let go and trust in God. They demonstrate that sometimes even death is truly beautiful.' – Andrea Hayes, 'Letting Go', October 2022

3. At night

Kind and Full of Mercy

I noticed a young girl getting on Dublin Bus and handing a five euro note to the driver. He told her they didn't take notes. It was maybe her first time on the bus in Dublin. She checked for change and didn't have enough. The driver could have told her to get off and get change. He just let her put what she had in and waved her on. This simple act of kindness stayed with me for a while.

Kindness is often simple or unrecognised, but it is what a lot of community, family and civic life is built on. It made me think of kindnesses I remembered from that day: someone sent me the web address for clothes I was looking for, and people were cleaning the paths along the canal near where I live. I was even happy that I had done a few kind acts that day. Most kindness is only remembered by the recipient: the text to someone lonely in lockdown or a phone call, the congrats for an exam passed, remembering an anniversary of marriage or death. It may be something more – like the loan or gift of money at a bad time. The one who is kind might not even notice how well it was appreciated.

Archbishop Michael Jackson, the Church of Ireland archbishop of Dublin, put it well speaking at the Festival of Eid al-Adha in Croke Park: 'Kindness is an act of every faithful person. It is a boomerang of love and of hope.' We are born to be kind. We grow in kindness with kindness given and received. It is a title often given to the Lord that he is kind and full of mercy.

As you look back on your day, can you remember a kindness you saw or experienced and give thanks to God for it?

Something to think and pray about tonight
I was born to be kind.

A word from the *Messenger*
'When you are kind you put others in the place of yourself. Self-love becomes unselfishness or out-going love. Are we not conscious of being loved when we experience true kindness? As Paul writes, "Love is kind" (1 Cor 13). Kindness can heal, lift us up and may even inspire us. This is not surprising as the impulse out of which kindness acts is the noblest part of ourselves.' – Aideen Madden, 'Kindness', December 2018

3. At night

Light in the Darkness

I have often heard of the 'dark love' of faith, but I knew very little of what it meant until a friend of mine, who was ninety-three years old, found herself praying for God to welcome her into the next life. She was terminally ill, and life was very difficult for her. She wondered why God was leaving her here. Had he forgotten her? As was her way, she battled to the end. Why did it happen this way?

One answer is that faith has its darkness. You can find that in the life of St Mother Teresa. She wrote privately of never finding peace and joy with God. Yet she believed in him, and spent her life in service of the poorest of the poor. Hers was a sort of dry love of God. Do you find you are the same? Perhaps someone you know and pray for struggles like that.

The question why is often a good prayer. Jesus prayed it: 'My God, my God, why have you forsaken me?' Once after a funeral, a mourner said to me, 'All I have now is faith. It is all so sad.' Is it only real faith when we do not understand? After all, if we understood, we wouldn't need faith. We often question why good people suffer before death. And there are other whys: the family left homeless, the refugees lost at sea, the hopes of friends dashed, people who are trying to escape addiction. Where is God?

God is your companion in darkness. God is the one who protects and cares for you. With all the suffering in the world, it sometimes appears as if God's hands are tied, fixed as they were when he was nailed to the cross. Your faith is tested. When there is nothing left but faith, however, you realise the true depth of your belief. Jesus said, 'What I say to you in the dark, tell in the light' (Mt 10:27). He encourages you to trust there is always light in darkness.

What have you found in the dark love of faith? Perhaps that God is near to you even when you feel he is absent. I have learned valuable lessons in failure, disappointment, loss and even sin. I have learned valuable ways of showing compassion and understanding to others, empathising with them. What you go through in darkness, many others go through too. It is a shared human experience that helps to grow your faith. Your darkness may one day shine a light for someone else.

Something to think and pray about tonight
God is my companion in darkness.

A word from the *Messenger*
'I suspect that for most of us our failures affect us in two ways. We grieve because we have let the Lord down, like Peter [when he denies Jesus], and we are disappointed in ourselves because we thought we were better than we are. The experience of Peter encourages us that our failures may actually serve to break our pride and lead us to a life of greater intimacy with and dependence on the Lord, who always seeks our reconciliation just as he did Peter's.' – David Breen, 'The Rehabilitation of Peter', May 2022

3. At night

Meaning

~~~

Exchanges with a hard-of-hearing colleague can be humorous at times. One went like this: I told him, as he was looking over the garden, 'You're like the lord of the manor.' He replied, 'I hope you enjoy the fruit.' What he had heard me say was 'I'm going to have a banana.'

A row at work over a small thing can be the result of a row at home earlier in the day. The teenager told to come home early may think 'early' means one in the morning! On many levels, people misunderstand one another. Even that lovely message 'I love you' can be heard in different ways.

The same is true of faith. People say they have lost their faith, when they mean they don't go to Mass anymore. Someone said to me, 'I don't pray anymore.' And then continued, 'I just talk to God in my own words.' What she meant was that she had given up the rote prayers she had learned as a child.

A friend once said to me, 'Please don't understand me too quickly.' That stuck with me. To find out what someone means, you need patience, a non-judgemental attitude and the realisation that all people are different. You need to pause and wonder what it is *they* mean. You need to hold onto the joy and adventure of getting to know someone. That in part is what Jesus means when he says, 'Just as I have loved you, you also should love one another' (Jn 13:34–35).

If you had trouble understanding someone today, try this tomorrow: reach out to them from a centre of love in your life; listen for the joy and pain in their words; notice their body language, their laughter and sighs; don't hear the words but miss the meaning.

Something to think and pray about tonight
Don't understand others too quickly.

A word from the *Messenger*
'Few of us are good listeners. In situations where active listening is called for one has to actively commit to listening. To listen well, one needs training and practice. It is true that not many of us have the ability to listen well, or maybe it is that we are so anxious to have our own opinions heard, to tell our story, that while the other person is speaking, the reply we intend to make is already being formulated in our minds. To give full attention we must empty our minds, maintain appropriate eye contact and be attuned to and able to interpret the facial expressions and body language of the speaker.' – Anne Marie Lee, 'Listening', January 2024

Surprise

In a group setting, I was asked to write my own Beatitudes. Another participant came up with 'Blessed are those who seek God, for they will be surprised.' I wish I had thought of that!

God is wider than any human experience. It makes sense then that God will often surprise you. You might be surprised by how much you are loved by others. Maybe you are struggling and your prayers have not been answered, and then help arrives in an entirely unexpected way. Maybe you are surprised by the fact that God wants to know you.

The biggest surprise of course is that God is immediately accessible in Jesus. I remember a schoolchild remarking to me, 'I want my God to have skin!' Children know things. 'I thank you, Father, Lord of heaven and earth, because you have hidden these things from the wise and the intelligent and have revealed them to children' (Mt 11:25).

God took human flesh, lived with joys and sorrows just like yours, did his best to help people and died in the hope of the Resurrection.

Whatever you went through today, remember that God is a God of surprises. God has been touched just as you have been touched, skin to skin. With such a God, you never know what surprise tomorrow will bring!

3. At night

Something to think and pray about tonight
God is wider than any human experience.

A word from the *Messenger*
'As a child I remember learning a prayer in Irish to the Sacred Heart: *A Chroí ró-Naofa Íosa, is asatsa atá mo mhuinín agam*, "O Sacred Heart of Jesus, I place all my trust in thee." I once saw this prayer as a tattoo on a man's arm. He was in prison, and he had it on his left arm, nearest to his heart, in memory of his mother, who had taught him the prayer as a child. It can be a surprise to encounter the signs of God's presence around us – even or rather especially in a prison cell.' – Fr John Cullen, 'God's Extravagant Love', June 2022

3. At night

Remembering the Dead

A preacher once said, 'I'm sure we all want to go to heaven. Hands up!' Everyone put up a hand. Then he added, 'Hands up those who want to go today!' No hand went up. Not surprising – the prospect of death is fearful.

Each time you pray the Hail Mary, you look ahead to death as you say, 'Now and at the hour of our death.' You remember the dead not only to pray for them, but to give thanks for their lives on earth and to draw hope from their present life with God. Belief in heaven is based on faith. There is no evidence of what it is like. 'We shall be like Christ' is one of the Apostles' phrases (1 Jn 1). While there is historical evidence that Jesus died, there is no on-the-spot evidence of the Resurrection. Historical records and even the tradition of the Shroud of Turin prove only that he died, not that he rose. Mary and the Apostles met him in a new way after the Resurrection. Still, it's what Christian faith is based on. Even when the Apostles saw him, they did not recognise him. Their recognition of him was more in his gift of consoling them, in familiar gestures like the breaking of bread and explaining the Scriptures.

In his *Spiritual Exercises*, St Ignatius Loyola says, 'Consider the office of consoling which Christ our Lord bears, and compare how friends are accustomed to consoling friends.' For St Ignatius, to console was more than sympathy; it also strengthened faith, hope and love and gave meaning to what seemed empty.

Because the Apostles knew Jesus that way, as a consoling friend, they had faith. When you remember and pray for loved ones who have died, they share with you something of the consoling grace of the Lord and of the new life they have with him. Tonight as you remember those who have died or look ahead to your own death, reach out to Jesus as a consoling friend.

Something to think and pray about tonight
Consolation strengthens faith, hope and love and gives meaning to what seems empty.

A word from the *Messenger*
'It is interesting to watch Jesus in the gospel stories, and how he is always out on the road, in consolation, meeting new situations and challenges, and responding in creative and loving ways. Consolation is essentially about the direction of travel or being on track: Am I moving towards God or away from God? Towards life, people and connection or into isolation, rumination and withdrawal? The key questions when facing difficulty are: What do I need to do to get back on track? How do I deal with the obstacle in my path? What will it take to solve this issue?'
– Brendan McManus SJ, 'How to Save Yourself from Despair', August 2025

A Smile

One icon of the Ascension has Jesus reaching heaven with a smile on his face. He has made it home after a long day! It is like getting out of a traffic jam and driving freely; like the joy of finding your lost keys; or, more seriously, like apologising to someone and knowing the freedom of forgiveness and like forgiving someone and not being bound by bitterness and grudges.

The Ascension is about getting somewhere after a long struggle. Jesus is no longer bound by time and space. Death cannot bind him to the earth or to the darkness. All is now eternity and light.

Could he not have left it like that? He could enjoy the rest of time without connections with the world or with God's people now? Could he not rest easy with his work well done, his Church ready for action and his mission accomplished? .

Our hope comes from the fact that Jesus is alive, is with us and is on our side. The angel said, 'Why do you look for the living among the dead?' (Lk 24:5). Hope doesn't come from within ourselves. It is a gift of God, to be prayed for and welcomed with thanks. Hope is being able to hum in the darkness and know we are not lost. It is to dig the garden, sure that next year's plants will grow. It is to look at our children and enjoy the future that stretches out before them. It is to be sure that love can grow in marriage and that life can go on and develop in our hearts even if love fades. It is the hope shared by the people who care tirelessly for loved ones, for the people who don't give up on a son or daughter in prison.

Our hope is sure because of Jesus. We are of sure hope because he was raised from death, and because he is with us all days. We are of sure hope because of the gift of faith within us, and we can joyfully say, 'Happy are we who have not seen but yet believe' (Jn 20:29). The smile of the ascending Lord Jesus can bring a smile to our face.

Something to pray and think about tonight
Jesus is alive, is with me and is on my side.

A word from the *Messenger*
'If asked "What are you hoping for?", what would you say? Let's take a moment to explore the inner world of our hopes. We have so many of them, lesser and greater. Without hope the world would be a very dull place. Everyone gets out of bed daily with hopes of some sort. Family living is packed with the challenge of immediate and longer-range hopes for the children. Animals too have hopes: think of the dog begging at the table. Hope is the energy that gets things going, and it is a gift of God. We are insatiable: hopes keep us alive, and we yearn for life to the full.' – Brian Grogan SJ, 'We're Bundles of Hopes', February 2025

Encouragement

Many years ago, I edited my first magazine. As a fifteen-year-old pupil, I took part in editing and writing the class magazines, *Forum* and *Agora* (with classical connotations). They included about twenty-five pages of articles and poems, contributed by the class. There were opinions on most areas of life, including what my classmates and I thought of politicians and even the Church. Fr John O'Hollohan, a Jesuit priest who was himself an editor and author, encouraged the class.

We didn't always get it right! Our work was checked for content, spelling and punctuation errors. Some of my opinions on the governing Fianna Fáil party were edited. The completed work was published and went out to interested parents, teachers and family members.

I wrote quite critical articles on the fortunes of the past pupils' rugby team! There was even an article on the class's proposed Irish rugby team, which was reprinted in the *Evening Press*.

All was the fruit of encouragement from teachers and fellow authors.

We are affected in many area of life by encouragement and praise. At home, one way of getting another selection of my mother's lovely cakes was to praise them. They would miraculously appear again.

A word of encouragement is worth a ton of exhortation! In sport we know the same: a shout of encouragement – 'Go on, you can do it' – is worth more than criticism.

St Paul knew that. He preached a lot but with words of encouragement also: 'I am being completely frank with you; I have great pride in you; I am filled with consolation; I am overjoyed in all our affliction' (2 Cor 7:4).

Some of his words of encouragement had a source in the encouragement Paul found in those he wrote to: 'I rejoice because I have complete confidence in you' (2 Cor 7:16)

Tonight, as you reflect on the day, try and find where God was encouraging you. God too rejoices in you, through all your afflictions, because he has 'complete confidence in you'.

Something to pray and think about tonight
God encourages me and has confidence in me.

A word from the *Messenger*
'Jesus told this parable [of the persistent widow] to encourage us to pray always and not give up in the face of a world that doesn't reflect God's intentions. The parable serves to assure us that, despite current circumstances and appearances, God's vindication will ultimately be ours on Christ's return. The widow's persistence in seeking justice serves as an inspiring example for us to continuously pray, 'Thy kingdom come, thy will be done on earth as it is in heaven.' – David Breen, 'The Widow and the Unjust Judge', July 2025

4: The Examen

The daily Examen is a prayer that Ignatius gave great importance to. If all prayers during the course of the day were to be missed, the Examen was the only one that must never be missed, Ignatius told his companions. Such were the benefits that Ignatius found in this simple but profound prayer. The Examen is a review of your day and has five parts to it.

This is a version of the five-step daily Examen that Ignatius practised.
1. Become aware of God's presence.
2. Review the day with gratitude.
3. How did I respond/How did I feel?
4. Choose one feature of the day and pray from it.
5. Look towards tomorrow.

Looking back over our day for about 5/10 minutes helps us to get in touch with where God was and where God is leading us. Ignatius describes this as 'my eyes were opened a little' as he slowly began to see how God loved him and where he was being guided in concrete ways during the day. This is what we are also invited to do as we review our day. When we see how we are loved by God and can experience it then everything changes. Ignatius believed this short practice of prayer was a gift from God.

4. The Examen

Step 1:
Become aware of God's presence with you now
Try to become aware of God's presence: 'I remind myself that in these moments, God is gazing on me with deep and unconditional love and holding me in being. I pause and think of this.'

Step 2:
Review your day with gratitude
Looking back over the course of your day, what are you grateful for? Try to be concrete about the things you are thankful for – maybe your family, job, good health, chat with a friend, happy memories, a walk in nature, the beauty of creation. Can you notice where God was present in all this? Can you see the gifts God has given this day? Even if the day was really difficult is there something you are thankful for?

Step 3:
How did I respond to the moments of my day/How did I feel?
Was I able to notice God's promptings during the moments of the day I have just recalled? Did I respond to people/situations in a good way or was it not so good? Did my heart feel warm and full or was it discouraged with little energy? Did God feel close or far away during my day? Did my responses help to build the relationships in my life (both human and divine)? If things didn't go too well today, remember how we are loved and held by God in all our brokenness and vulnerability. As we ask forgiveness, we are showered with love, healing and the grace to move forward.

Step 4:
Choose one feature from the day and pray from it
Was there one encounter/situation/person that was particularly positive or challenging for me today? Bring this time to God now and talk openly and freely about it and how it was for you. Trust that God is interested in this and offers love, peace and healing to you.

Step 5:
Look towards tomorrow
As you come to the end of your prayer from today, look ahead to tomorrow and invite God to be with you in all the day will bring. If there is something particular that you have planned – a meeting, appointment, trip or maybe another day just by yourself – ask God to be with you in it. Our God is a God of relationship. What's important to us, is important to God. As in the words spoken to Jeremiah 31:3: 'I have loved you with an everlasting love; therefore I have continued my faithfulness to you.'

Notes from my morning prayer

Notes from my morning prayer

Notes from my daytime prayer

Notes from my daytime prayer

Notes from my nighttime prayer

Read about the Church of today and the Church of the future

- Pope's intention
- Prayer and reflections
- Care for the Earth
- The Church around the world
- Social justice

Plus Re:Link for schools, crosswords, cookery and much, much more!

The Sacred Heart
MESSENGER
September 2025 €2.50/£2.15

A modern message in a much-loved tradition since 1888

Happy Birthday Mary!
Tom Casey SJ

Quiet Faith
Fr Gerard Condon

Back to School
Anne Marie Lee

Since 1888

Subscribe Now

to Ireland's most popular religious magazine

Digital or Postal subscriptions available.
Subscriptions start from only €15!

Contact: 01-6767491
or www.messenger.ie

Messenger MJP Publications